Using Google Earth™:
Bring the World into Your Classroom

Level 6-8

Author

JoBea Holt, Ph.D.

The author would like to thank her family for all their support, ideas, and critical reviews.

Publishing Credits

Dona Herweck Rice, *Editor-in-Chief;* Robin Erickson, *Production Director;* Lee Aucoin, *Creative Director;* Timothy J. Bradley, *Illustration Manager;* Sara Johnson, M.S. Ed., *Senior Editor;* Hillary Wolfe, *Editor;* Tracy Edmunds, *Associate Education Editor;* Corinne Burton, M.A.Ed., *Publisher*

Standards

©2004 Mid-continent Research for Education and Learning (McREL)
©2007 Teachers of English to Speakers of Other Languages, Inc. (TESOL)

Shell Education

5301 Oceanus Drive
Huntington Beach, CA 92649-1030
http://www.tcmpub.com
ISBN 978-1-4258-0826-6
© 2012 Teacher Created Materials, Inc.

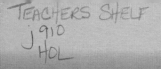

Table of Contents

Research and Introduction

No matter how hard you look, you will never find Oz, Neverland, or Narnia on a map. But, if you know where to look and what to look for, you will find the great Mississippi River where Minn and Huck Finn traveled, the prairies and woods where Laura and Caddie grew up, and San Nicolas Island where Karana and Rontu became friends. You may discover that Minn and Huck passed by the starting point for Lewis and Clark's expedition, only at a different time, or that Karana eventually was rescued and taken to the mission in Santa Barbara. Or, you may discover that Laura's family moved from their little house on the prairie because it was in Indian Territory, or that your grandmother lives where Caddie played.

Using Google Earth™: Bring the World into Your Classroom introduces students to Google Earth, and more importantly, to Earth itself. There is so much Earth can tell us about the landscapes where explorers traveled, the settings in classic children's literature, and how the forces of nature shape our planet's surface.

Objectives

There are several objectives for *Using Google Earth™: Bring the World into Your Classroom*:

1. To introduce students to children's literature, social studies, mathematics, and Earth science through a very visual experience.

2. To add an exciting geographic dimension to reading, social studies, mathematics, and science.

3. To create student-generated maps that link students' personal worlds to the worlds of literature, science, mathematics, and social studies.

4. To allow students to build a Google Earth™ folder system to record where they travel in their reading adventures, social studies lessons, and in their personal experiences.

5. To encourage project-based learning and authentic tasks.

6. To align with national standards in social studies, science, mathematics, language arts, geography, and technology.

"Geography is an integrating discipline that helps students understand, participate in, and make informed decisions about the world around them" (Shultz et al. 2008). By using images of Earth as an integrating force, literature, social studies, mathematics, and science flow together. "The interactive nature of virtual globes can facilitate learning through an enjoyable and individually-oriented session..." (Shultz et al. 2008). The ability to use a three-dimensional model of Earth facilitates understanding of the Earth system and the many subject areas that it comprises, from science, to history, to art, or any topic with a geographic component (SERC 2009). Plus, research suggests that when technology is integrated throughout the curriculum, students will not only learn technology skills but also content (Silverstein et al. 2000).

Research and Introduction *(cont.)*

Teaching with Technology

Using Google Earth encourages the teacher to step out of a traditional lecture-based mode of teaching and into the role of facilitator or coach as students navigate through the program. Cognitive research shows that learning improves when students are actively involved in learning, working in groups, frequently interacting and receiving feedback, and seeing the connections to real life (Roschelle et al. 2001). One goal of this resource is to show students (and teachers) that this technology is more than just a fun tool—it provides an access point for content-area instruction. "It is important to remember that teaching students how to use the program is not enough. Think about why the students are using the program. What project can they accomplish? What question or problem can they solve when they use the program to create a product?" (Frei, Gammill, and Irons 2007). *Using Google Earth™: Bring the World into Your Classroom* offers students an entry way into the curriculum that is broad, authentic, and engaging. And the more students practice functioning in creative, integrated, collaborative learning domains across all the content areas, the better (Bean 2010).

Because Google Earth is inherently engaging and maneuverable, it is a natural fit for interactive whiteboards and computer use in classrooms. Students will learn to see Earth in new ways and to explore and develop stories about what they discover. According to the Project New Media Literacies (Card, Mackinlay, and Shneiderman 1999), maps offer students opportunities for visualization, and better visualization makes us smarter. "Google Maps/Earth are helping us tell stories better and bringing geographic data to life in ways that make traditional maps look more like decorations on the wall" (Castiglione 2009). With this resource, students can build a growing set of maps that record their adventures in books and in class, and tie these adventures to their family histories and personal experiences.

Google Earth and Reading

Through Google Earth, teachers can also incorporate informational text into their lessons from sources such as *TIME*® *for Kids*, NASA's *Earth Observatory* website, and *National Geographic* magazine. Reading informational text is a key initiative from the Common Core Curriculum Standards for Language Arts, especially in terms of analyzing key ideas and details, and the integration of knowledge and ideas (Common Core State Standards 2010). By tying informational text to a real-world setting, and then having students experience that location in an authentic visual way, they are able to add dimension to the details described in the text, as well as build schema as they integrate new information into their existing understanding of the world.

Overview of Google Earth

Images from Space

The first picture of Earth was not inspiring. It was taken in 1946 by a 35mm camera on a V-2 missile at an altitude of 65 miles and was very fuzzy. Perhaps the most important image of Earth taken by the National Aeronautics and Space Administration (NASA) is called Earthrise—an image captured in 1968 on Apollo 8, the first manned mission to orbit the Moon, by astronaut Bill Anders. He said, "We came all this way to explore the Moon, and the most important thing is that we discovered the Earth." The first Earth Day soon followed.

NASA continues to take images of Earth, but now focuses on using a variety of instruments operating at a wide range of wavelengths in order to measure our atmosphere, land surface, and oceans.

A suite of NASA satellites continuously monitors key factors that help scientists understand our water, energy, and biological cycles. To see these datasets in detail, visit http://earthobservatory.nasa.gov/GlobalMaps/.

Image courtesy of NASA's Astronomy Picture of the Day website: http://antwrpagegsfc.nasa.gov/apod/ap101115.html

Astronaut Tracy Caldwell Dyson enjoys the view from the International Space Station's window

However, ask any astronaut what they spend their spare time doing in orbit, and most will say they spend it looking out the window of the Space Shuttle or the International Space Station, watching Earth go by. Their photographs are one of their most valued treasures from their missions, and all are available for us to see. Visit the Gateway to Astronaut Photography of Earth's website at http://eol.jsc.nasa.gov/. The best and most relevant images are presented on NASA's Earth Observatory (http://earthobservatory.nasa.gov/), a website that keeps us informed of dynamic and timely events with daily images of Earth.

Image courtesy of NASA's Astronomy Picture of the Day website: http://apod.nasa.gov/apod/ap081224.html

"Earthrise" photograph from Apollo 8, the first manned mission to orbit the moon

Overview of Google Earth *(cont.)*

What Is Google Earth ?

Google Earth is both a data set and a software tool.

Data Set

The data set consists of thousands of high-resolution images of our planet taken from space that have been mosaicked together onto a globe. The global mosaic primarily contains cloud-free images of the highest resolution. In some cases, however, nearby images can look quite different if they have been taken in a different season, at a different time of day, or with a different instrument.

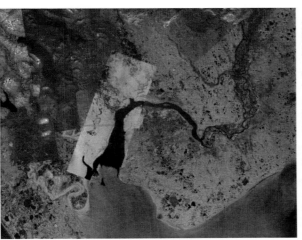

Image ©2010 TerraMetrics, ©2010 Google, Data SIO, NOAA, U.S. Navy, NGA, GEBCO, ©2010 Europa Technologies

A view of southern Alaska showing images from a variety of seasons, sun angles, and instruments.

Images from past times, going back to the 1940s, can also be accessed using Google Earth in some locations. Some of these are black and white and many are of much lower resolution than the latest versions, but all can tell us something about how our planet has changed. Many of the Google Earth images have been taken by NASA instruments on satellites in polar orbits.

Software Tool

The second part of Google Earth is the software that allows users to explore the mosiacked images. This software operates through the Internet to allow a user to "fly" to any place on Earth at almost any resolution without keeping a high-resolution global data set on his or her computer.

In 2010, NASA flew an instrument called Shuttle Radar Topography Mission (SRTM) on the Space Shuttle. The instrument used two imaging radar antennas configured to measure the topography of the entire land surface between the latitudes of 60° north and south in only 11 days. This digital topographic data set has been layered on top of the Google Earth image globe to provide Google Earth 's 3D capabilities.

Most recently, several organizations, including the U.S. Navy and the National Oceanic and Atmospheric Administration (NOAA), have provided ocean data to Google Earth. This capability is rapidly being enhanced to allow users to explore beneath the surface of the sea.

How to Use This Book

Using Google Earth™: Bring the World in Your Classroom was created by a former NASA scientist to provide teachers with a manageable way to access this technology in the context of content-area lessons, and use the features in the images to teach students about the history and sciences of our planet. Each lesson introduces and demonstrates one or more Google Earth tools within a simple, easy-to-follow format, always keeping the standard as the focus of the lesson.

The first three units of this resource introduce students to the basic features of Google Earth. The first unit introduces students to the Earth in the **3D viewer**, the **navigation tools**, and the **Search**, **Places**, and **Layers panels**. The lessons are organized to build student competency with Google Earth. The second unit teaches students how to see natural, artificial, and abstract features on Earth and provides a means of referencing the scale of features they are seeing. The third unit shows students how to save and organize the places they visit so that these places can be compared to places students visit in the future.

In the remaining five units, students will learn to explore our planet in Google Earth in the context of content-area lessons, including language arts, social studies, science, and mathematics, as well as a cross-curricular unit that includes space exploration, the oceans, Earth at night, and new discoveries.

The information on pages 8–12 outlines the major components and purposes for each activity and pages 14–21 detail how to prepare for instruction. Page 13 gives a visual reference of the main Google Earth tools used in this book.

How to Use This Book (cont.)

Lesson Plan

Standard shows the geography objective addressed in the activity. Content-area lessons address the subject-specific standard in addition to geography.

Google Earth Tools are listed here. Tools introduced in the lesson are denoted with an asterisk. Use the *Google Earth Reference Window* on page 13 and the Teacher Resource CD (Reference.pdf) to familiarize yourself with the locations of the various tools.

Vocabulary words and **Materials** are shown here.

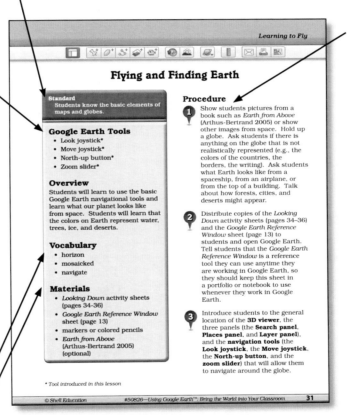

Procedure, a step-by-step description of the lesson, is shown here. It is recommended that teachers work through the procedure for each lesson in Google Earth and preset all placemarks before presenting the lesson to students.

How to Use This Book (cont.)

Lesson Plan (cont.)

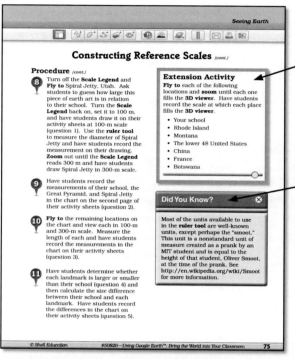

Extension Activities provide opportunities for independent practice, or allow teachers to add more dimension or provide additional challenges.

Did You Know? offers related information and fun facts to help students make connections across content areas and activate their prior knowledge.

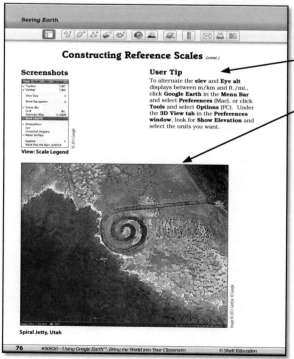

User Tips offer technical advice or shortcuts.

Screenshots provide a visual frame of reference.

How to Use This Book *(cont.)*

Lesson Plan
(cont.)

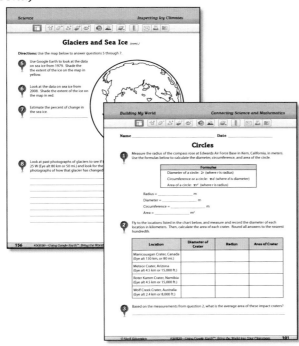

Student Activity Sheets assess students' content knowledge as well as their Google Earth technology skills. Answer keys are provided in Appendix B (pages 224–233), and an Assessment Rubric Guide is available in Appendix C (pages 234–235), and on the Teacher Resource CD (Tech_Rubric.pdf).

The **Teacher Resource CD** contains reproducible copies of all the student activity pages and additional teacher resources. See Appendix H for a list of CD contents (pages 253–254).

How to Use This Book *(cont.)*

Preparing for Lessons

Before presenting each lesson, work through the lesson yourself in Google Earth and **placemark** each location. Then, when you are presenting to the class, you can double-click on each **placemark** in the **Places panel** to fly directly to each location.

Google Earth Reference Window

Distribute copies of the **Google Earth Reference Window** to students at the beginning of the first lesson. Make a copy for yourself as well or enlarge it and display it in the classroom. This visual reference will be very helpful in identifying **Google Earth Tools** as you work through the lessons.

Lesson Presentation

The **Procedures** in each lesson describe how to manipulate Google Earth on a projected screen or interactive whiteboard in front of students. Students can observe Google Earth on the screen or whiteboard and fill out their activity sheets.

Depending on your classroom setup, there are a number of alternative ways to present the lessons:

• Ask individual students to manipulate Google Earth using the class computer or interactive whiteboard during the lessons.

• If students have their own computers or small groups of students can share computers, they can follow along through each step of the lesson.

• Present part of the lesson to students as a group and then let them complete the activity sheets using their computers.

The **Extension Activities** are designed to be completed by individual students or small groups of students after they have received instruction in the main lesson.

Google Earth Reference Window

Toolbar

Placemark
Polygon
Image Overlay
Path
Tour
Clock
Sun
Planets
Email
Ruler
Print
View in Google Maps™

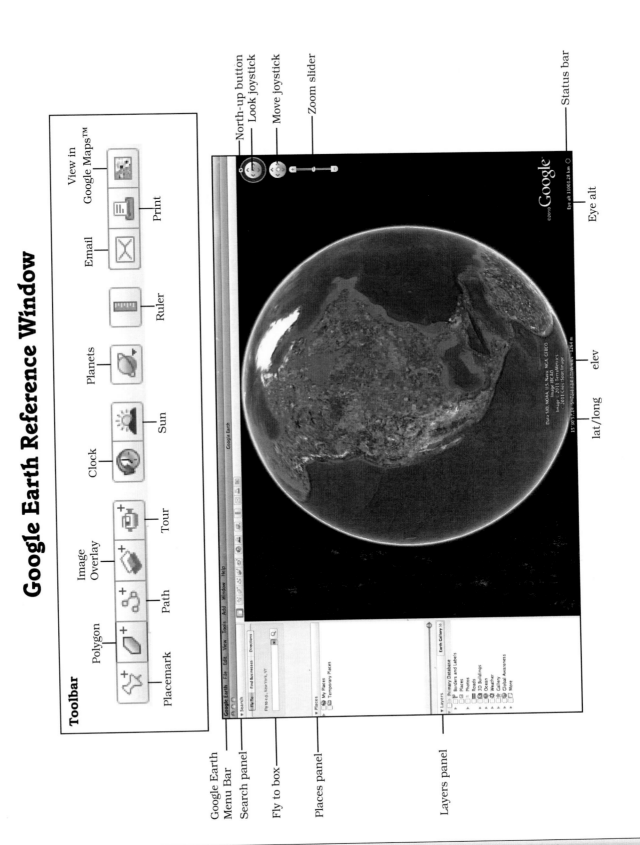

Google Earth Menu Bar
Search panel
Fly to box
Places panel
Layers panel

North-up button
Look joystick
Move joystick
Zoom slider
Status bar
Eye alt
elev
lat/long

Preparing for Google Earth Instruction *(cont.)*

Preparing the Technology

Exploring with Google Earth requires a computer, access to the Internet (preferably through a direct line connection), and display technology in your classroom.

1. System Requirements

Google Earth runs on both PCs and Macs. System requirements to run Google Earth 6.0 for Macs and PCs and video card requirements are shown here:

System Requirements

PC	Mac
Minimum: • Operating System: Windows XP, Windows Vista, or Windows 7 • CPU: Pentium 3, 500Mhz • System Memory (RAM): 256 MB • Hard Disk: 400MB free space • Screen: 1024 × 768, "16-bit High Color" DirectX9 (to run in Direct X mode) • Graphics Card: Direct X9 and 3D capable with 64 MB of VRAM • Network speed: 128 Kbits/sec	**Minimum:** • Operating System: Mac OS X 10.5.0 or later • CPU: Any Intel Mac • System Memory (RAM): 256 MB • Hard Disk: 400MB free space • Screen: 1024 × 768, "Thousands of Colors" • Graphics Card: Direct X9 and 3D capable with 64 MB of VRAM • Network speed: 128 Kbits/sec
Recommended: • Operating System: Windows XP, Windows Vista, or Windows 7 • CPU: Pentium 4, 2.4GHz+ or AMD 2400xp+ • System Memory (RAM): 512 MB • Hard Disk: 2GB free space • Screen: 1280 × 1024, "32-bit True Color" • Graphics Card: Direct X9 and 3D capable with 256 MB of VRAM • Network speed: 768 Kbits/sec	**Recommended:** • Operating System: Mac OS X 10.5.2 or later • CPU: Dual Core Intel Mac • System Memory (RAM): 512 MB • Hard Disk: 2GB free space • Screen: 1280 × 1024, "Millions of Colors" • Graphics Card: Direct X9 and 3D capable with 256 MB of VRAM • Network speed: 768 Kbits/sec

Note: A version of Google Earth is available for the iPad™, but it does not include many of the features used in these lessons.

Preparing for Google Earth Instruction *(cont.)*

Preparing the Technology *(cont.)*

2. Internet Requirements

High-speed Internet is required to run Google Earth. The minimum speed required is 128 Kbits/sec and the recommended speed is a minimum of 768 Kbits/sec.

Google Earth requires a large amount of bandwidth to run. If you are using a wireless connection, the screen may freeze and Google Earth will need to be restarted. If the problem persists, try connecting directly to your router via an ethernet cable. Full resolution views of the most recent places you visited are saved temporarily on your computer's cache, and can be replayed from the hard drive without connecting to the Internet.

Some school sites use Internet blockers or firewalls which can interfere with Google Earth content.

3. Display Technology for Flexible Grouping

The optimum means to display Google Earth is to use an interactive whiteboard or a projector with your computer. Students may interact with the program by coming up to the board or by pressing the appropriate keys on the teacher's computer keyboard. Alternately, small groups of students may gather around a single computer and work through the lessons together. If you are using this resource in a lab where students each have access to a computer, students may observe as the teacher introduces the lesson, and then continue to work through the lesson at their own stations.

4. Maintaining Student and Classroom .kmz Files

Students have the opportunity to develop files that record their adventures in the Google Earth file format called Keyhole Markup Language (**.kml**). Most files in Google Earth use the extension **.kmz**, which stands for KML-zipped. Ideally, students will maintain these **.kmz files** throughout their school careers. Given that students may do some of their work on school computers and some on home computers, students may choose to keep their working **.kmz files** on a memory stick. Instruct students on how to also maintain a backup file on their home or classroom computer in case the memory stick is lost. Ensure students save their entire **.kmz file** at the end of the school year so that it is ready to augment the following year.

Preparing for Google Earth Instruction *(cont.)*

Setting Up Google Earth

Google Earth is a program that can be downloaded from the Internet for free. To use the program, you must have access to the Internet with the specifications outlined on page 14.

1. **Download Google Earth**

    Open your Internet browser, go to http://earth.google.com, click on "Download Google Earth," and then "Agree and Download." Look for the .dmg file on your desktop or in your download folder (Mac) or the .exe file (PC) and click on it to install it. Follow the directions for installing Google Earth on your computer. If you use a Mac, find Google Earth in your **Applications** folder and drag it to your dock. If you use a PC, find Google Earth in your **Programs** file and create a shortcut on your desktop.

Open Google Earth by double-clicking on the Google Earth icon in your dock or desktop. *Note:* If the "Tip" window opens, click the button that says you no longer want this window and close it. You will see the **3D viewer** (a picture of Earth with the sky in the background) on the right, and three panels titled **Search**, **Places**, and **Layers** on the left. You are now ready to explore!

Note: Keep a copy of the *Google Earth Reference Window* near your keyboard as you begin to explore in Google Earth. Give each student a copy to use as they learn new tools, or enlarge the *Google Earth Reference Window* and post it where it will be visible to all and easily referenced during lessons.

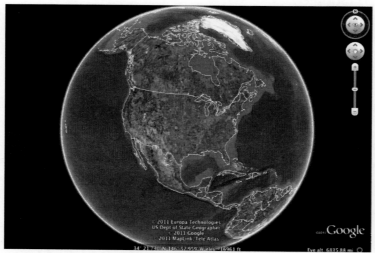

3D viewer in Google Earth

Preparing for Google Earth Instruction *(cont.)*

Setting Up Google Earth *(cont.)*

2. Set Your Preferences

To access the **Preferences** settings on a Mac, click on **Google Earth** in the **Google Earth Menu Bar**, and choose **Preferences** from the dropdown menu. On a PC, click on **Tools**, then **Options**, and choose **Google Earth Options** from the dropdown menu to open the **Preferences window**. Set your Google Earth preferences to match the screenshots that follow.

Choose "Feet, Miles" or "Meters, Kilometers"

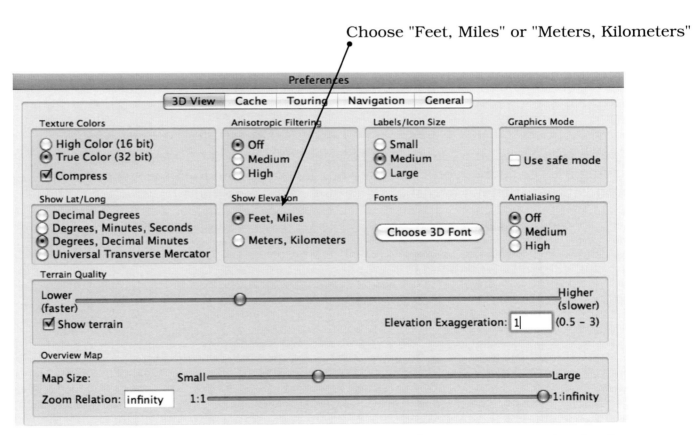

Preferences Window: Set preferences for texture colors, icon sizes, standard or metric measurements, fonts, terrain quality, and map size.

Preparing for Google Earth Instruction *(cont.)*

Setting Up Google Earth *(cont.)*

2. Set Your Preferences *(cont.)*

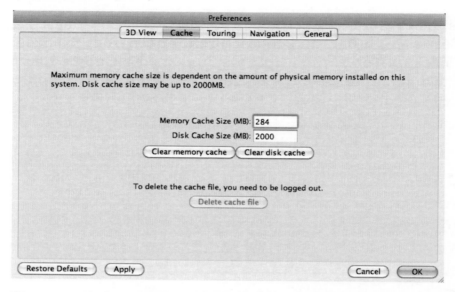

Cache tab: You can make the cache size as large as 2,000 MB (2 Gigabytes). By having a large cache, you can save your latest Google Earth views and find them even without Internet access.

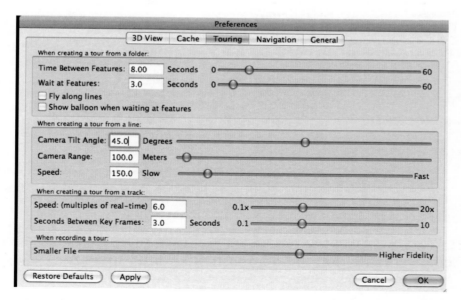

Touring tab: Adjust the settings for touring. Try to keep the speeds low enough so students can keep track of where they are going.

Preparing for Google Earth Instruction *(cont.)*

Setting Up Google Earth *(cont.)*

2. Set Your Preferences *(cont.)*

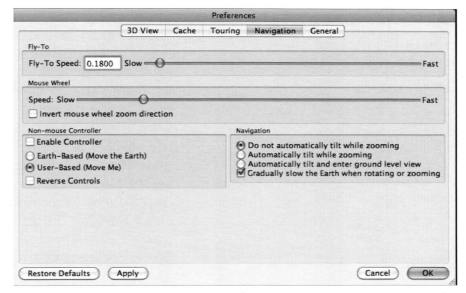

Navigation tab: Change settings for "flying" speeds and set preferences for tilt and ground level views.

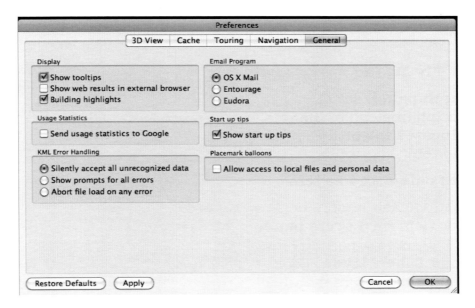

General tab: Set your display preferences and choose the appropriate email program you wish to access for sending files. Select whether to see user tips every time Google Earth starts, and allow your **placemarks** compatibility with other files and data.

Preparing for Google Earth Instruction *(cont.)*

Setting Up Google Earth *(cont.)*

3. Set the View Menu

In the **Google Earth Menu Bar** across the top of the screen, click on **View** and turn on the following options:

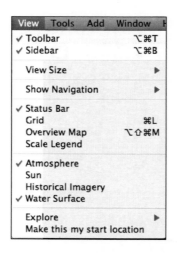

4. Select the Fly To Tab

In the **Search panel,** select the **Fly To tab** (instead of the **Find Businesses tab** or the **Directions tab**).

5. Turn Off Folders and Layers

Before starting each lesson, be sure all layers in the **Layers panel** are turned off, except perhaps the **Borders and Labels layer**. Look through your **Places panel** and turn off any **placemarks** that are not relevant to your lesson. Or, leave the **placemarks** turned on to compare places your class has visited.

6. Apply Google SafeSearch™

Make sure that Google SafeSearch is set to *strict filtering* as Google Earth will provide students with access to the Internet. Open the Google home page (http://www.google.com/) and look in the upper right corner for the **gear icon**. Click the **gear icon** and select *Search Settings*. Look for *SafeSearch Filtering* and select *Use strict filtering (Filter both explicit text and explicit images)*. Then, click **Save Preferences** to save.

Preparing for Google Earth Instruction *(cont.)*

Important Technology Notes

Using the Mouse

Lesson procedures often call for right-clicking with the mouse. If you have a single-click mouse or a trackpad, you can use control-click to accomplish the same function.

Finding Locations

Some locations may be tricky to find in Google Earth. Before using the **Fly to box** to search for a specific location, first navigate to the general area of the Earth. Always preview each location before presenting a lesson to students.

Printing

Images from Google Earth should be printed at a high resolution, but color printing can be expensive. Consider saving images as PDFs and displaying your images onscreen rather than printing them.

Updating Google Earth

Like any evolving technology, Google Earth is constantly updating their application and services. Always make sure you have the most up-to-date version downloaded, and install updates regularly. Depending on the version you use, tools and commands may be found in slightly different locations on the screen than what is described in this resource.

Google Earth is contantly updating the layers data. If any of the layers used in these lessons do not appear in the **Layers panel**, search in the **Google Earth Gallery** for the missing layers.

Getting Help

The How-to Guide in Appendix D of this book (pages 232-238) contains instructions for using most Google Earth tools. For additional help, see the online Google Earth Support pages (http://earth.google.com/support). Google Earth is fairly intuitive, and in most cases, the online resource will be able to help you solve your problem.

Differentiation

Why Differentiate?

To successfully differentiate instruction, teachers must first know their students. Teachers must determine the readiness levels of students, as well as take into consideration the type of support they may need. It is important to make adjustments in the curriculum when students are having trouble with the material. Finding new ways to present information, using manipulatives or realia, and providing opportunities for targeted support are important aspects of a differentiated classroom.

Below are some reasons why and ways to differentiate the curriculum for diverse learners using this resource.

- **Content:** Vary the content (what is being taught or the materials students will use) when students are not at the same academic readiness level.

- **Process:** Vary the process (how it is taught or what amount of support you provide students) when you have students with diverse learning styles or readiness levels.

- **Product:** Vary the product (what students produce) when you have students with a variety of different readiness levels, interests, and passions.

Using *Google Earth™: The World in Your Classroom* offers a tremendous opportunity for differentiation with an authentic and engaging way to capture student interest and have them connect to the material. The interactive nature of Google Earth requires students to engage in higher-order thinking skills as they analyze what they see, apply their knowledge of locations to new settings, synthesize the information they discover, and evaluate the effects of social and environmental conditions on geography. This is an inherent differentiation strategy built into the lessons because all students will approach these tasks and questions at their own readiness and ability levels.

Content

When using this resource with below-level learners and English language learners, key vocabulary terms are called out so that they may be introduced before each activity. Provide graphic organizers or word banks to scaffold instruction. In addition, each lesson offers an **Extension Activity** for above-level learners. Use these activities to encourage more in-depth investigation of a topic or to ask students to apply the skills they have learned in an alternate setting or situation.

Differentiation *(cont.)*

Why Differentiate? *(cont.)*

Process

The lessons in *Google Earth™: The World in Your Classroom* offer students the ability to participate in authentic tasks with real-world applications. By exploring and investigating Earth, students are actively engaged in discovery learning, inquiry-based learning, and authentic problem-solving. Students can work in flexible group arrangements, with partners, in small groups, or individually. The **Extension Activities** suggest ideas for students to complete independent investigations, and can be modified for below-level students or English language learners to be completed in pairs or small groups. The lessons can be slowed down or sped up depending on the readiness levels of the students, as well.

Product

The activities in *Google Earth™: The World in Your Classroom* appeal to students' varying interests. Students draw, write, and research. They build models, interact with technology, and use kinesthetic methods to experience and retain information. Tier the products in the lessons and assign appropriate products to match student readiness levels. Allow above-level students to extend their learning by creating more challenging products as a result of the lessons. For example, students can create visual art based on what they saw in Google Earth, or create and narrate an interactive presentation.

Additional Differentiation Strategies

The research-based strategies above can be used to differentiate the content, process, and product (Conklin 2011) of this resource. The next section offers a brief definition of each strategy.

Differentiation *(cont.)*

Strategies for Working with English Language Learners

Google Earth offers a truly visual and experiential way to see Earth, investigate science, uncover mathematical concepts, participate in history, and become immersed in literature—a practical resource for diverse learning styles. For English language learners, this tool provides incredible support and access to the curriculum.

Nevertheless, it is appropriate to provide additional scaffolds to these learners. Here are some ways to support the English language learners in your classroom.

1. **Use visual media as an alternative to written responses.**

   The activities in this book offer options for students to sketch or capture screenshots or use pictures in their answers.

2. **Frame questions to make language accessible.**

   When possible, provide word banks and introduce key vocabulary before completing the activities. This will help students use new words in context. Sentence frames or question frames can also make the language more accessible. Some examples include:

   - Would it be better if...?
   - How is_____ related to _____?
   - Why is _____ important?
   - Why is _____ better than _____?

3. **Give context to questions to enable understanding.**

   Use pictures and icons to help students recall key instructions and vocabulary. The activities in this book include **screenshots** to help provide visual references, and the icons are highlighted as well.

4. **Provide sentence frames or stems to encourage higher-order thinking.**

   Providing language tools will help students express what they think and will help you get the information you are looking for. In addition, these frames will provide models for oral language responses. Some examples include:

   - This is important because...
   - This is better because...
   - This is similar to...
   - This is different from...
   - I agree/disagree with _____ because...
   - I think _____ because...

Standards Correlations

Shell Education is committed to producing educational materials that are research- and standards-based. In this effort, we have correlated all of our products to the academic standards of all 50 United States, the District of Columbia, the Department of Defense Dependent Schools, and all Canadian provinces. We have also correlated to the Common Core State Standards.

How to Find Standards Correlations

To print a customized correlation report of this product for your state, visit our website at http://www.shelleducation.com and follow the on-screen directions. If you require assistance in printing correlation reports, please contact Customer Service at 1-877-777-3450.

Purpose and Intent of Standards

Legislation mandates that all states adopt academic standards that identify the skills students will learn in kindergarten through grade twelve. Many states also have standards for Pre-K. This same legislation sets requirements to ensure the standards are detailed and comprehensive.

Standards are designed to focus instruction and guide adoption of curricula. Standards are statements that describe the criteria necessary for students to meet specific academic goals. They define the knowledge, skills, and content students should acquire at each level. Standards are also used to develop standardized tests to evaluate students' academic progress. Teachers are required to demonstrate how their lessons meet state standards. State standards are used in the development of all of our products, so educators can be assured they meet the academic requirements of each state.

McREL Compendium

We use the Mid-continent Research for Education and Learning (McREL) Compendium to create standards correlations. Each year, McREL analyzes state standards and revises the compendium. By following this procedure, McREL is able to produce a general compilation of national standards. Each lesson in this product is based on one or more McREL standards. The chart on pages 26-29 lists each standard taught in this product and the page number(s) for the corresponding lesson(s).

TESOL Standards

The lessons in this book promote English language development for English language learners. The standards listed on page 30 support the language objectives presented throughout the lessons.

Standards Correlation (cont.)

Lesson Title	Content Area	Standard
Flying and Finding Earth (pages 31–36)	Geography	Students know the basic elements of maps and globes.
Searching for Schools (pages 37–42)	Geography	Students know the similarities and differences in various settlement patterns of the world.
Placemarking Egypt (pages 43–48)	Geography	Students know the location of physical and human features on maps and globes.
Layering Landmarks (pages 49–54)	Geography	Students know how places and regions serve as cultural symbols.
Identifying Artificial Geographic Features (pages 55–60)	Geography	Students know how technology shapes the human and physical characteristics of places (e.g., satellite dishes, computers, road construction).
Investigating Natural Geographic Features (pages 61–66)	Geography	Students know how landforms are created through a combination of constructive and destructive forces.
Overlaying Abstract Geographic Features (pages 67–72)	Geography	Students know the purposes and distinguishing characteristics of different map projections, including distortion on flat-map projections.
Constructing Reference Scales (pages 73–78)	Geography	Students know the relative location of, size of, and distances between places (e.g., major urban centers in the United States).
Sorting with Folders (pages 79–84)	Geography	Students understand the characteristics and uses of maps, globes, and other geographic tools and technologies.
Planning an Imaginary Trip (pages 85–90)	Geography	Students understand the characteristics and uses of maps, globes, and other geographic tools and technologies.

Standards Correlation *(cont.)*

Lesson Title	Content Area	Standard
Making Literature and Social Studies Connections (pages 91–96)	Social Studies	Students understand the forces of cooperation and conflict that shape the divisions of Earth's surface.
Connecting Science and Mathematics (pages 97–102)	Geography	Students know the locations of places, geographic features, and patterns in the environment.
	Mathematics	Students understand formulas for finding measures.
Charting the Setting of a Book (pages 103–108)	Geography	Students understand how physical systems affect human systems.
	Language Arts	Students know the defining features and structural elements of a variety of literary genres.
Watching Events Unfold (pages 109–114)	Geography	Students know the ways in which changes in people's perceptions of environments have influenced human migration and settlement over time.
	Language Arts	Students understand complex elements of plot development.
Touring a Book (pages 115–120)	Geography	Students understand the physical and human characteristics of place.
	Language Arts	Students use a variety of resource materials to gather information for research topics.
Creating a Book Report (pages 121–126)	Geography	Students know the ways in which changes in people's perceptions of environments have influenced human migration and settlement over time.
	Historical Understanding	Students make basic oral presentations to the class.
Experiencing the News (pages 127–132)	Geography	Students know the effects of natural hazards on human systems in different regions of the United States and the world.
	Social Studies	Students know about life in urban areas and communities of various cultures of the world at various times in their history.

Standards Correlation *(cont.)*

Lesson Title	Content Area	Standard
Tracking Pizarro (pages 133–138)	Geography	Students understand the characteristics and uses of spatial organization of Earth's surface.
	Social Studies	Students understand characteristics of the Spanish and Portuguese exploration and conquest of the Americas.
Mapping the Roman Empire (pages 139–144)	Geography	Students understand the physical and human characteristics of place.
	Social Studies	Students understand influences on the economic and political framework of Roman society.
Going Back in Time (pages 145–150)	Geography	Students understand that culture and experience influence people's perceptions of places and regions.
	Social Studies	Students understand and know how to analyze chronological relationships and patterns.
Inspecting Icy Climates (pages 151–156)	Geography	Students know the causes and effects of changes in a place over time.
	Science	Students know features that can impact Earth's climate.
Colliding Plates (pages 157–162)	Geography	Students know how landforms are created through a combination of constructive and destructive forces.
	Science	Students know that the Earth's crust is divided into plates that move at extremely slow rates in response to movements in the mantle.
Shading the Earth (pages 163–168)	Geography	Students understand concepts such as axis, seasons, rotation, and revolution (Earth-Sun relations).
	Science	Students know how the tilt of the Earth's axis and the Earth's revolution around the Sun affect seasons and weather patterns.
Using Energy (pages 169–174)	Geography	Students understand the origins and environmental impacts of renewable and nonrenewable resources, including energy sources like fossil fuels.
	Science	Students know the processes that produce renewable and nonrenewable resources.

Standards Correlation *(cont.)*

Lesson Title	Content Area	Standard
Measuring America (pages 175–180)	Geography	Students understand the characteristics and uses of spatial organization of Earth's surface
	Mathematics	Students use proportional reasoning to solve mathematical and real-world problems
Building a Capital (pages 181–186)	Geography	Students understand the symbolic importance of capital cities.
	Mathematics	Students understand geometric transformation of figures.
Adding Up Algebra (pages 187–192)	Geography	Students know how human activities have increased the ability of the physical environment to support human life in the local community, state, United States, and other countries.
	Mathematics	Students understand and apply basic and advanced properties of functions and algebra.
Subtracting the Amazon (pages 193–198)	Geography	Students know the causes and effects of changes in a place over time.
	Mathematics	Students select and use appropriate estimation techniques.
Exploring Mars (pages 199–204)	Geography	Students know that astronomical objects in space are massive in size and are separated from one another by vast distances.
Migrating with Whales (pages 205–210)	Geography	Students know ways in which organisms interact and depend on one another through food chains and food webs in an ecosystem.
Oberserving Population (pages 211–216)	Geography	Students understand distributions of physical and human occurrences with respect to spatial patterns, arrangements, and associations.
Discovering Places (pages 217–222)	Geography	Students understand the ways in which technology influences the human capacity to modify the physical environment.

Standards Correlations (cont.)

TESOL Standards

Lesson	Content Area	Standard
All lessons	All content areas	To use English to communicate in social settings: Students will use English to participate in social interactions
All lessons	All content areas	To use English to communicate in social settings: Students will interact in, through, and with spoken and written English for personal expression and enjoyment
All lessons	All content areas	To use English to communicate in social settings: Students will use learning strategies to extend their communicative competence
All lessons	All content areas	To use English to achieve academically in all content areas: Students will use English to interact in the classroom
All lessons	All content areas	To use English to achieve academically in all content areas: Students will use English to obtain, process, construct, and provide subject matter information in spoken and written form
All lessons	All content areas	To use English to achieve academically in all content areas: Students will use appropriate learning strategies to construct and apply academic knowledge
All lessons	All content areas	To use English in socially and culturally appropriate ways: Students will use the appropriate language variety, register, and genre according to audience, purpose, and setting
All lessons	All content areas	To use English in socially and culturally appropriate ways: Students will use nonverbal communication appropriate to audience, purpose, and setting
All lessons	All content areas	To use English in socially and culturally appropriate ways: Students will use appropriate learning strategies to extend their sociolinguistic and sociocultural competence

Flying and Finding Earth

Standard
Students know the basic elements of maps and globes.

Google Earth Tools
- Look joystick*
- Move joystick*
- North-up button*
- Zoom slider*

Overview
Students will learn to use the basic Google Earth navigational tools and learn what our planet looks like from space. Students will learn that the colors on Earth represent water, trees, ice, and deserts.

Vocabulary
- horizon
- mosaicked
- navigate

Materials
- *Looking Down* activity sheets (pages 34-36)
- *Google Earth Reference Window* sheet (page 13)
- markers or colored pencils
- *Earth from Above* (Arthus-Bertrand 2005) (optional)

* Tool introduced in this lesson

Procedure

 1 Show students pictures from a book such as *Earth from Above* (Arthus-Bertrand 2005) or show other images from space. Hold up a globe. Ask students if there is anything on the globe that is not realistically represented (e.g., the colors of the countries, the borders, the writing). Ask students what Earth looks like from a spaceship, from an airplane, or from the top of a building. Talk about how forests, cities, and deserts might appear.

 2 Distribute copies of the *Looking Down* activity sheets (pages 34–36) and the *Google Earth Reference Window* sheet (page 13) to students and open Google Earth. Tell students that the *Google Earth Reference Window* is a reference tool they can use anytime they are working in Google Earth, so they should keep this sheet in a portfolio or notebook to use whenever they work in Google Earth.

 3 Introduce students to the general location of the **3D viewer**, the three panels (the **Search panel**, **Places panel**, and **Layer panel**), and the **navigation tools** (the **Look joystick**, the **Move joystick**, the **North-up button**, and the **zoom slider**) that will allow them to navigate around the globe.

Flying and Finding Earth (cont.)

Procedure (cont.)

4 To turn or rotate Earth in the **3D viewer**, click and hold on a location on the Earth and move the mouse to drag the it in the direction of your choice. Look for an ocean, a desert, a forest, an island, and an ice- and snow-covered region. On their activity sheets, ask students to describe each region using descriptive adjectives related to color, shape or texture, and to include their feelings or impressions about the feature (question 1).

5 Move the Earth using the cursor and show students that North can be anywhere in the **3D viewer**. Most people are more comfortable seeing North at the top of the globe. Show students that as you turn Earth, the *N* on the **North-up button** rotates as well. Use the cursor to move the **North-up button** or click on the *N* to return North to the top.

6 Turn Earth until Africa is in full view with *N* at the top of the **North-up button**. On their activity sheets, direct students to color Africa with colored pencils, using the same colors that appear in Google Earth. Ask them to label a desert, an island, a forest, and an ocean (question 2). Have students describe what the colors might represent on the Google Earth globe (question 3).

7 Point to the **zoom slider** below the **Look joystick** and **Move joystick**. Show students how the **zoom slider** can move the view closer or farther away. You can also use the scroll wheel on the mouse to **zoom** in or out. **Zoom** in and out to illustrate the different resolutions available for viewing.

8 Use the cursor and the **North-up button** to rotate Earth so North America is in view and North is at the top of the viewer. Rotate the Earth until you are over a large city (New York City, New York; San Francisco, California; or another large city with which you are familiar). **Zoom** in until you recognize familiar features (Central Park in New York City or the Golden Gate Bridge in San Francisco), and point these out to students.

9 Click on the **Move joystick** and ask students to call out the cardinal direction in which you move as you press each arrow.

Flying and Finding Earth *(cont.)*

Procedure *(cont.)*

10 **Zoom** in until buildings in the city are in clear view. Click and hold the small arrow at the top of the **Look joystick** until Earth's horizon is in view. Have students describe on their activity sheets how this view of Earth is different from a view from above (question 4). Click and hold the small arrow at the bottom of the **Look joystick** or type *u* on the keyboard to return Earth to a view from above.

Screenshot

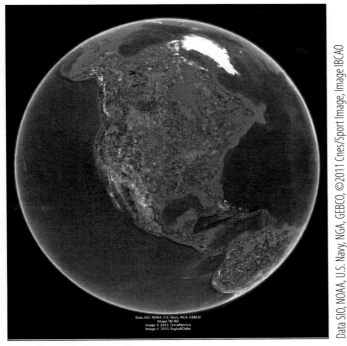

Earth in the 3D viewer

Data SIO, NOAA, U.S. Navy, NGA, GEBCO, ©2011 Cnes/Spot Image, Image IBCAO

Extension Activities

- Have students choose a different continent, color it, and label the major forests, deserts, islands, and ice- and snow-covered regions.
- Tell students to use the **navigation tools** to investigate the coast of Greenland, the Sahara Desert, or a Greek island. Have students describe what they see or anything that surprises them.

Did You Know? ⊗

In Google Earth, the pictures of the globe are made using images taken by advanced instruments and cameras on satellites in space. The images are mosaicked together like a puzzle to provide complete coverage of the globe. If an area was pieced together with several images, students may see different lighting effects or colorations and may confuse these with natural or man-made boundaries.

Name_____ Date _____

Looking Down

1 Describe the regions that you see using descriptive adjectives for each column in the chart.

Feature	Color	Shape or Texture	Feeling or Impression
desert			
island			
forest			
ocean			
ice- or snow-covered area			

Looking Down *(cont.)*

 2 Color the globe below using the same colors that appear in Google Earth. Label a desert, a forest, an island, and an ocean.

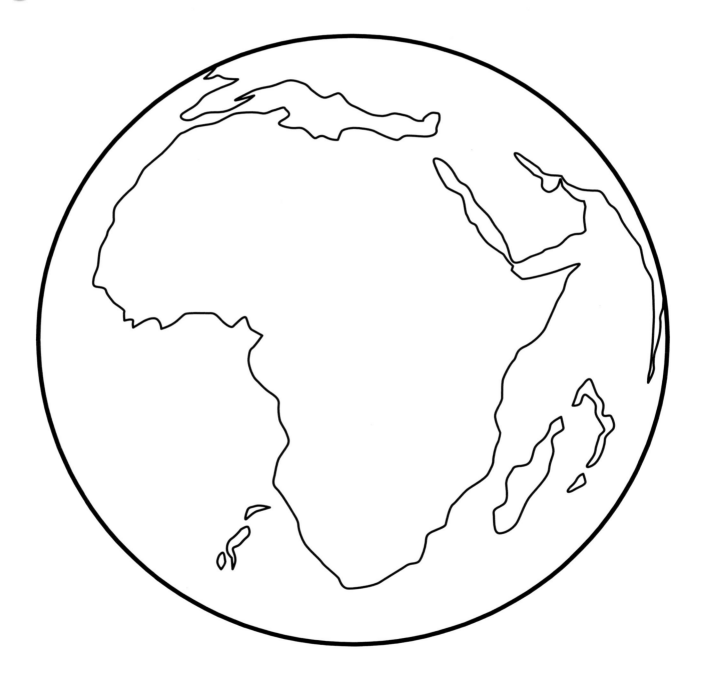

Looking Down *(cont.)*

3 On the lines below, describe what each color might represent on the Google Earth globe.

green _____

blue _____

brown _____

tan _____

white _____

4 Zoom in close to the surface of Earth. Click and hold the small arrow at the top of the Look joystick until Earth's horizon is in view. Describe how this view of the Earth is different from the view from above.

_____

_____

_____

_____

_____

_____

Searching for Schools

Standard
Students know the similarities and differences in various settlement patterns of the world.

Google Earth Tools
- Search panel: Fly to box*

Overview
Students will continue to learn to use the basic Google Earth tools by searching for and exploring their own school and schools around the world.

Vocabulary
- rural
- suburban
- urban

Materials
- *Schools Around the World* activity sheets (pages 41–42)

* Tool introduced in this lesson

Procedure

 1 Distribute copies of the *Schools Around the World* activity sheets (pages 41–42) to students and open Google Earth. (***Note:*** Make sure the **Fly To tab** is selected in the **Search panel**, not the **Businesses** or the **Directions tabs**).

 2 On their activity sheets, have students describe characteristics of rural, suburban, and urban environments (question 1). For example, a rural environment has open spaces and fewer buildings. An urban environment has more buildings. A suburban environment often has more homes placed in an organized pattern.

 3 Type the name of your city or town with the state, province, or country (e.g., Phoenix, Arizona; Paris, France) in the **Fly to box**, click the magnifying glass or press the "Enter" key, and Google Earth will navigate to that location. (You may see red balloon **icons** in the **Search panel** listing different locations. Double-click on the location you would like to go to and Google Earth will navigate to that location.) Point out familiar locations to orient students. Ask students to decide if they live in a rural, urban, or suburban environment, and to defend their decisions by listing specific details that they see in Google Earth (question 2).

Searching for Schools *(cont.)*

Procedure *(cont.)*

4 Tell students that schools in different communities look different, too, based on the type of community in which they are found. Tell students they will look at different schools and see how they are similar to or different from their own school.

5 Type your school address in the **Fly to box**, including the city, state or province, and country, and click the magnifying glass. On their activity sheets, have students write the address of their school (question 3). **Zoom** in to a view that allows you to point out familiar features, such as sports fields, parking lots, school buses, or buildings to orient students. Ask students to write down three features or places that they recognize (question 4).

6 **Fly to** Taipei, Taiwan, and wait for Google Earth to navigate to this location. Then type "Junior High School" in the **Fly to box** and click the magnifying glass or press Enter. Double-click the **balloon icon** next to "Nan Man Junior High" in the **Search panel**. **Zoom** in and investigate the school. Have students write the name of the school and city in the first circle of the Venn diagram on their activity sheets and add a description of the school and the area around the school, including whether it is in a rural, urban, or suburban area (question 5).

7 **Fly to** Colorado Springs, Colorado. Once there, search for "Jenkins Middle School" using the **Fly to box**. **Zoom** in and investigate the school. Have students write its name and city in the second circle of the Venn diagram on their activity sheets and add a description of the school and the area around the school.

8 **Fly to** Blantyre, Malawi. Once there, search for "Blantyre Secondary School." **Zoom** in and investigate the school and have students write its name and city in the third circle of the Venn diagram on their activity sheets, along with a description of the school and the area around the school.

9 Have students compare the three schools and complete the Venn diagram.

10 Have students write a paragraph comparing their school to one of the schools they investigated (question 6).

Searching for Schools *(cont.)*

Extension Activity

Ask students to describe a typical day in their lives. What do they do after school? **Fly to** the locations where these things happen, using Google Earth. Ask students to imagine they are attending one of the schools they investigated. How would their lives be different? Have them write a short essay describing a typical day in the life of a student attending one of these schools.

User Tip

Sometimes typing just the name of a famous place in the **Fly to box** is enough to find that place. Other times, you need to add the city, state, or country. In most cases, you will need to use your **navigation tools** to provide a recognizable and interesting view.

When looking for a specific location, **Fly to** the general area first, then search for the exact place you want to see.

Did You Know?

Universities in the United States are easy to recognize in Google Earth because of the concentration of sports fields. **Fly to** the University of California, Berkeley, CA; Princeton University, Princeton, NJ; and Ohio State University, Columbus, OH. Identify the football, tennis, and baseball fields at each university.

Searching for Schools *(cont.)*

Screenshots

Image ©2011 DigitalGlobe, Image ©2011 GeoForce Technologies

Nan Man Junior High, Taipei, Taiwan

©2010 Google

Blantyre Secondary School, Malawi

Image ©2011 DigitalGlobe

Jenkins Middle School, Colorado Springs, Colorado

Name_____ Date _____

Schools Around the World

1 Describe some characteristics of the types of communities listed below.

Location	Characteristics
Rural	
Urban	
Suburban	

2 Fly to your city or town. What type of community do you live in? List the specific details that you see in Google Earth that support your assertion.

_____

_____

_____

3 Write the address of your school below.

_____

4 What are three features of your school that you recognize in Google Earth?

_____

_____

_____

Schools Around the World *(cont.)*

5 Use the triple Venn diagram below to describe the similarities and differences between the schools you viewed in Google Earth.

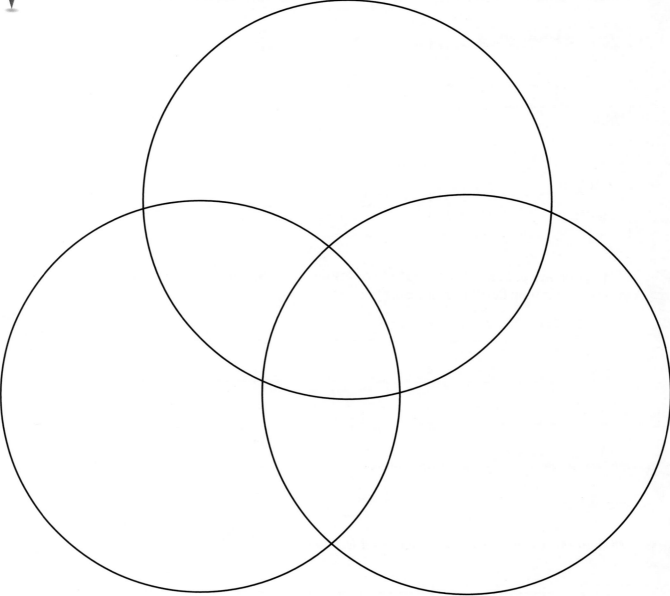

6 On a separate sheet of paper, write a paragraph comparing your school to one of the schools you investigated.

Placemarking Egypt

Standard
Students know the location of physical and human features on maps and globes.

Google Earth Tools
- Places panel: Folders*
- Toolbar: Placemark*

Overview
Students will continue to learn to use Google Earth tools by exploring the Nile River in Egypt and its role in a developing civilization. They will learn about the importance of a river to a culture.

Vocabulary
- delta
- floodplain
- irrigation
- sparse

Materials
- *The Gift of the Nile* activity sheets (pages 46–48)
- chart paper
- markers or colored pencils

Procedure

 1 Ask students to name necessary geographical components for stable civilizations. List their responses on chart paper in order of importance. Lead students to see that a water source and naturally irrigated land are of prime importance.

 2 Distribute copies of *The Gift of the Nile* activity sheets (pages 46–48) to students and open Google Earth.

 3 **Fly to** Egypt. **Zoom** in and identify the Nile River and the Nile Delta. **Zoom** in just below the Nile Delta until the Nile River comes into view. Look more closely at the river and the areas surrounding the river. On their activity sheets, ask students to describe the river and indicate in which direction the water flows (question 1).

 4 Tell students they can save the places they visit by adding a **placemark**. Direct students to the third page of their activity sheets that includes detailed explanations of how to set and modify **placemarks**. Tell students that in this lesson you will model how to set **placemarks** and later they can use these directions to set **placemarks** on their own.

* Tool introduced in this lesson

Placemarking Egypt *(cont.)*

Procedure *(cont.)*

5 Click on the **placemark tool** (a yellow thumbtack) in the **Toolbar** at the top of the **3D viewer** (see the *Google Earth Reference Window* on page 13). A **placemark icon** with a flashing square around it will appear in the **3D viewer** along with a **placemark window**.

6 Drag the **placemark icon** to a location on or near the Nile River. Type "Nile River, Egypt" in the **Name box** in the **Placemark window** and click **OK**. Look for the **placemark** in the **Places panel** or **Search panel** and use the cursor to drag it to the **My Places folder** in the **Places panel** to store it for the next time you open Google Earth on the same computer.

7 Point out the floodplain where the river floods annually. Discuss why the floodplain was and still is important to Egyptian agriculture. Look for evidence of agriculture (e.g., green, geometric-shaped fields) in the floodplain and delta.

8 Show students how the delta fans out before reaching the Mediterranean Sea. Then, **zoom** out to see the desert surrounding the Nile River and compare it to the green areas in the floodplain. **Zoom** in and look at several places where the floodplain ends and the desert begins.

9 On their activity sheets, ask students to write a definition of a delta and a floodplain (question 2). Have students color and label the delta, the floodplain, and the desert on the diagram (question 3).

10 Point out how the population becomes sparser farther from the floodplain. Ask students to brainstorm how these more distant communities get access to water (question 4).

11 **Fly to** the Great Pyramid of Giza, Egypt, and **placemark** the pyramid. Then, follow the edge of the floodplain south to look for the remains of other pyramids and tombs near the meeting point of the desert and the floodplain. **Placemark** several of these sites.)Directions for setting and modifying placemarks are shown on page 48 of the student activity sheet.) Ask students to look at the locations of these pyramids and tombs. **Zoom** out to view all the pyramid **placemarks**. Have students write about why they think the pyramids and tombs were built on the edge of the Nile floodplain (question 5).

Placemarking Egypt *(cont.)*

Extension Activity

Investigate the floodplains around other rivers where early civilizations developed, such as the Indus River (Harappa, Pakistan); the Ganges River (Koyra, Bangladesh); and the Tigris and Euphrates Rivers (Baghdad, Iraq). Ask students how these areas compare to the Nile River. (***Note:*** The Tigris and Euphrates rivers are used extensively for irrigation, so their floodplains are more difficult to distinguish.)

User Tips

Placemarks can only be moved or edited when their **Placemark window** is open. To move or edit a **placemark**, right-click (or control-click) on the **placemark** and choose **Get Info** (Mac) or **Properties** (PC) to open the **Placemark window**.

Sometimes, when you name a placemark, the placemark name reverts to **Untitled Placemark** after you save. To avoid this, click once in the **Description box** before closing the **Placemark window**.

Use the cursor to drag **placemarks** to the **My Places folder** in the **Places panel** to save them so they appear every time your computer is turned on. **Placemarks** left in the **Search panel** will be deleted when Google Earth is closed.

Screenshot

©2011 Cnes/Spot Image, Data SIO, NOAA, U.S. Navy, NGA, GEBCO, Image
©2011 DigitalGlobe, Image U.S. Geological Survey

The Nile River and the Nile Delta

Name_____ Date _____

The Gift of the Nile

1 Describe the Nile River on the lines below. Which direction does the water flow?

_____

_____

_____

2 Write definitions for the terms below.

delta: _____

floodplain: _____

3 Color and label the delta, floodplain, and desert on the map below.

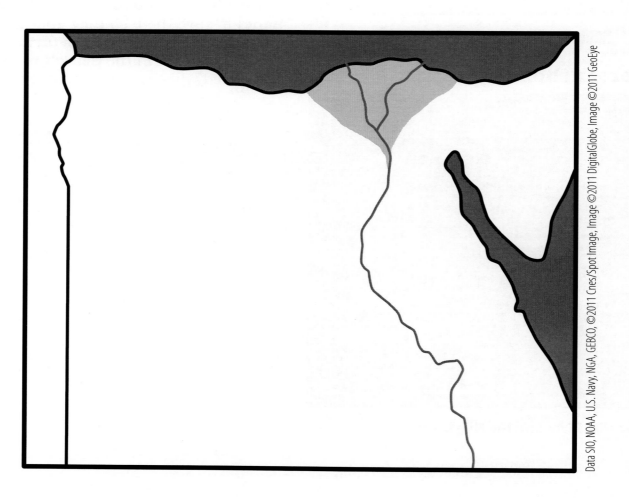

The Gift of the Nile *(cont.)*

4 As you navigate west of the floodplain, notice how the population becomes sparser. How do you think these more distant communities get access to water?

_____

_____

_____

_____

5 Placemark the site of the Great Pyramid of Giza. Move south and look for the remains of other pyramids and tombs along the edge of the desert where it meets the floodplain. Placemark several of these locations. Zoom out to look at all the placemarks. Why do you think the ancient Egyptians chose to build pyramids and tombs in these areas?

_____

_____

_____

_____

_____

_____

_____

_____

_____

_____

_____

The Gift of the Nile *(cont.)*

Setting and Modifying Placemarks

To set a placemark:

1. Click on the placemark tool (a yellow thumbtack) in the Toolbar at the top of the 3D viewer. A yellow thumbtack placemark icon with a flashing square around it will appear in the 3D viewer and a placemark window will open.

2. Drag the placemark icon to the location of your choice and type a name in the name box in the placemark window. Click on the Style, Color tab to modify the color and size of the placemark icon and label. To change the look of the placemark icon, click on the yellow thumbtack in the upper right corner of the placemark window. A placemark icon window will appear where you can select any number of placemarks, or choose "No Icon" if you want to label a placemark with just a name. When you are finished customizing the placemark, click OK to close the placemark window.

3. Look for the placemark in the Search panel or the Places panel and drag it to the My Places folder. It will now appear every time your computer is turned on. Placemarks left in the Search panel will be deleted when Google Earth is closed.

To move or modify a placemark:

1. Placemarks can only be moved or modified when their placemark window is open. To move or edit a placemark, right-click (or control-click) on the placemark in the Search panel or Places panel and choose Get Info (Mac) or Properties (PC) to open the placemark window.

2. Drag the placemark icon in the 3D viewer to move it. Make any desired changes in the placemark window and click OK to close the placemark window and save the placemark.

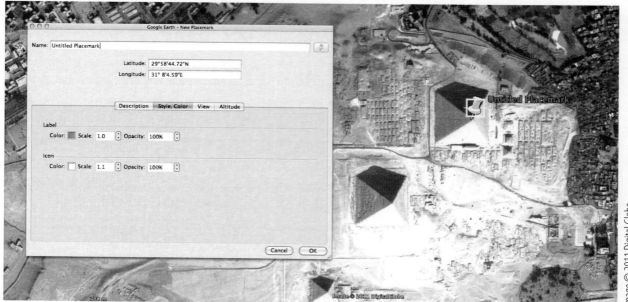

Layering Landmarks

Standard
Students know how places and regions serve as cultural symbols.

Google Earth Tools
- Layers panel: 3D Buildings*
- Layers panel: Photos*
- Layers panel: Roads*
- Layers panel: More: Wikipedia*
- Toolbar: Placemark

Overview
Students will learn to use the Layers panel to identify cultural symbols and landmarks around the world and to use Google Earth to access online articles.

Vocabulary
- icon

Materials
- *Cultural Symbols* activity sheets (pages 52–54)

Procedure

1 Distribute copies of the *Cultural Symbols* activity sheets (pages 52–54) to students and open Google Earth.

2 **Fly to** the Golden Gate Bridge, San Francisco, California. **Zoom** in and center the bridge in the **3D viewer**. Ask students if they can identify a toll booth, the towers, and the cars. **Placemark** the bridge.

3 Tell students that in this lesson you will demonstrate some of the different data layers available in Google Earth. Direct students to the third page of their activity sheets (page 54) for detailed information on using the **Layers panel**.

4 In the **Layers panel**, click the box next to **Photos** to turn on the **Photos layer**. When the layer is turned on, the box will be checked. Click on some of the **photo icons** that appear around the bridge in the **3D viewer** to see photos taken in the area. Have students describe the bridge on their activity sheets using what they see in the photos (question 1). Turn off the **Photos layer** by unchecking the box next to **Photos**.

* Tool introduced in this lesson

Layering Landmarks *(cont.)*

Procedure *(cont.)*

5 **Fly to** the Syndey Opera House, Sydney, Australia. Turn on the **3D Buildings layer** in the **Layers panel**. **Zoom** in near the Opera House and use the **Look joystick** to see the 3D model. Have students write a description of the Opera House (question 2).

6 In the **Layers panel**, turn off the **3D Buildings layer**. Click on the arrow or plus sign next to the **More layer** to open it. Then, turn on the **Wikipedia layer**. Click on the **Wikipedia icon** on the Sydney Opera House in the **3D viewer**. Have students use the information in the pop-up window to answer questions 3 and 4. Turn off the **Wikipedia layer**.

7 **Fly to** the Washington Monument, Washington, DC, and **placemark** it. Turn on the **3D Buildings layer**, **zoom** in, and use the **Look joystick** to view the model of the monument. Have students write a description of the monument (question 5). Turn off the **3D Buildings layer** and and type *u* on the keyboard to return to an overhead view.

8 **Zoom** out to view the National Mall and turn on the **Places layer**. Hover the cursor over the **place icons** around the National Mall. Have students list some of the icons and write what each one represents (question 6).

9 Turn on the **Wikipedia layer**. Have students work with partners to investigate an article about one of the monuments or museums on the National Mall and summarize what they learned on their activity sheets (question 7). Ask students to share something they learned about why the monument or museum they investigated is an important symbol.

10 **Fly to** London, England, then **Fly to** the London Eye and the Houses of Parliament. **Placemark** each location. Turn on the **3D Buildings layer**, **zoom** in, and use the **Look joystick** to view the 3D model of the London Eye. Turn off the **3D Buildings layer** and return to an overhead view. Turn on the **Roads layer** and ask students to write down the roads they would take to get from the London Eye to the Houses of Parliament (question 8).

Extension Activity

Navigate to a view of the lower 48 United States and turn on the **Roads layer** and the **Borders and Labels layer**. **Zoom** in until the highways appear. What major Interstate highways go through Chicago? Have students investigate why Chicago is an important city for highways.

Layering Landmarks *(cont.)*

Screenshots

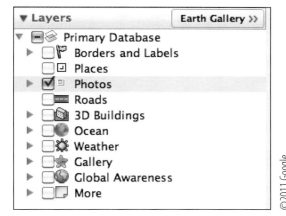

©2011 Google

Photos layer in the Layers panel

©2011 Google

London Eye 3D model, London, England

©2010 Google

Golden Gate Bridge, San Francisco, California with Photos layer

Name_____ Date _____

Cultural Symbols

1 Fly to the Golden Gate Bridge, San Francisco, California. Look at the bridge using the Photos layer and describe the bridge and the surrounding area.

_____

_____

_____

_____

2 Fly to the Sydney Opera House, Sydney, Australia and look at the 3D model. Describe the Opera House.

_____

_____

_____

_____

3 Turn on the Wikipedia layer. Click on the Wikipedia icon on the Sydney Opera House and read the information in the pop-up window. What prize for architecture did the architect receive?

_____

4 Do you think the architect deserved this prize? Why or why not?

_____

_____

_____

_____

_____

_____

Cultural Symbols *(cont.)*

5 Fly to the Washington Monument, Washington, DC and look at the 3D model. Describe the monument.

_____

_____

_____

_____

6 Look at some of the place icons surrounding the National Mall in Washington, DC. List some of the place icons and explain what each one represents.

_____

_____

_____

_____

_____

_____

7 With a partner, use the Wikipedia layer to read an article that explains more about one of the monuments or museums on the National Mall in Washington, DC. Then, summarize what you learned on the lines below.

_____

_____

_____

_____

_____

8 Fly to the London Eye, London, England, and then the Houses of Parliament, London, England. Turn on the Roads layer. Write the names of the roads you would take to get from the London Eye to the Houses of Parliament.

_____

_____

_____

Cultural Symbols *(cont.)*

Using the Layers Panel

The Layers panel, located in the lower-left corner of the Google Earth window, contains many data sets that can be overlaid in Google Earth.

• To turn on a layer and make it appear in the 3D viewer, click the small box to the left of the layer. You will see a check mark in the box when the layer is turned on. To turn a layer off, click the box again to remove the checkmark.

• Some layers have sublayers within the layer. To see the sublayers, click the small arrow (Mac) or the plus sign (PC) to the left of the layer. This will display sublayers in that menu. Some sublayers have sublayers as well.

• When some layers are turned on, they display small icons in the 3D viewer that are hard to see or find. Double-click on a layer in the Layers panel and Google Earth will navigate to a view in which you can see and click on the icons associated with that layer.

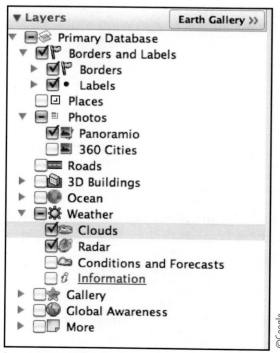

Layers panel

Identifying Artificial Geographic Features

Standard
Students know how technology shapes the human and physical characteristics of places (e.g., satellite dishes, computers, road construction).

Google Earth Tools
- Layers panel: 3D Buildings
- Layers panel: Roads
- Status bar: Eye alt*
- Toolbar: Placemark

Overview
Students will investigate artificial, or man-made, geographic features.

Vocabulary
- altitude
- geographic features
- sea level

Materials
- *Artificial Evidence* activity sheets (pages 58–60)

Procedure

1. Tell students that the surfaces of planets are made of geographic features. Many planets have natural geographic features like mountains, volcanoes, and craters. Abstract geographic features like latitude and longitude lines can be used on any planet. Earth, however, has extensive artificial geographic features, like buildings and bridges.

2. Distribute copies of the *Artificial Evidence* activity sheets (pages 58–60) to students and open Google Earth. On their activity sheets, have students sort the natural or artificial features into columns (question 1). Ask students to name some specific examples of artificial features (question 2).

3. Turn off all layers and places in the **Layers panel** and the **Places panel**. **Zoom** out to the smallest view of Earth. Show students the **Eye alt** display in the **Status bar** at the bottom of the **3D viewer**. Tell students that **Eye alt** indicates the altitude of your eye above the surface of Earth. Specifically, it is the height of your eye above sea level at the center of the **3D viewer**. It should currently be about 64,000 km (40,000 mi.), which is only about $\frac{1}{6}$ the distance to the Moon.

* Tool introduced in this lesson

Identifying Artificial Geographic Features *(cont.)*

Procedure *(cont.)*

4 One feature that many people believe is visible from space is the Great Wall of China. **Fly to** Badaling Zhen, YanQing, Beijing, China and **zoom** to an **Eye alt** of 10 km (30,000 ft.). Look about 4 km (2.5 mi.) to the east for two tree icons indicating the Great Wall. Turn on the **3D Buildings layer** and you will see the Great Wall running along the mountain ridges. Center a section of the Great Wall in the **3D viewer**. **Placemark** the section. Move the **placemark** to the **Places panel** and turn off the **3D Buildings layer**.

5 **Zoom** out slowly until it is no longer possible to see the Great Wall. Ask students to write on their activity sheets the **Eye alt** at which the wall is no longer visible (question 3).

6 Students' activity sheets list the **Eye alt** of a typical passenger airplane, the International Space Station, and the Apollo lander on the Moon. Tell students to use this information to answer question 4.

7 Other artificial features on Earth include structures that have been built for science, exploration, transportation, communication, sports, religion, recreation, or novel living spaces. **Fly to** the structures listed in question 5 on students' activity sheets and **zoom** in and out to note the highest **Eye alt** at which students can see each structure. Have students use this information to determine which structures can be seen from the International Space Station (question 5).

8 Sometimes the addition of an artificial feature has a major impact on the surrounding environment. **Fly to** Novo Progresso, Brazil, and turn on the **Roads layer** in the **Layers panel**. **Zoom** in until highway BR163 appears. Investigate the highway, its location, and the surrounding area.

9 Have students work with a partner to write a paragraph about the impact of building this highway in the Amazon forest (question 6).

Did You Know? ⊗

The Moon, Mars, and even Venus have landers and rovers on them that were sent there by people on Earth to explore. A picture of an artificial geographic feature on the Moon can be seen here: http://apod.nasa.gov/apod/ ap110908.html.

Identifying Artificial Geographic Features *(cont.)*

Extension Activity

Choose any country and use the **Move joystick** to navigate across it at an **Eye alt** of about 9.5 km (30,000 ft.) Look for areas that have no artificial geographic features. Have students make one list of regions with many artificial geographic features, and another list of regions with few artificial geographic features. What is the relationship between population and artificial geographic features?

Screenshots

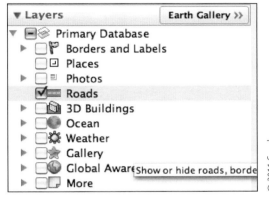

Roads layer in the Layers panel

© 2011 Google

Image ©2011 DigitalGlobe, ©2011 Mapabc.com, ©2011 Europa Technologies

The Great Wall at Badaling, China

Name_____ Date _____

Artificial Evidence

1 Sort the features in the word bank into the correct columns.

Word Bank			
lake	canal	river	town
bridge	crop	road	volcano
building	reservoir	trail	

Natural Features	Artificial Features

2 Name some specific examples of artificial features (e.g., the Golden Gate Bridge or Hoover Dam).

_____

_____

_____

_____

_____

_____

Artificial Evidence *(cont.)*

3 Zoom out slowly from the Great Wall of China. Write the Eye alt at which the wall is no longer visible.

Eye alt: _____

4 Look at the altitudes of the objects below. Write *yes* or *no* to show if you think the Great Wall of China would be visible from each height.

Eye alt of a typical passenger airplane = 9.5 km (30,000 ft.) _____

Photo courtesy of NASA

Eye alt of the International Space Station = 275 km (170 mi.) _____

Image courtesy of NASA, http://apod.nasa.gov/apod/ap101010.html

Eye alt of Apollo on the Moon = 400,000 km (250,000 mi.) _____

Artificial Evidence *(cont.)*

 Using Google Earth, locate the structures listed in the chart below. Zoom out until each is no longer visible. In the second column, write the highest Eye alt at which the structure is still visible. In the third column, indicate whether the structure would be visible from the International Space Station.

Structure	Highest altitude when the feature was still visible	Visible from International Space Station? (yes or no)
Arecibo Observatory, Arecibo, Puerto Rico		
John F. Kennedy Space Center, Florida		
Palm Islands, Dubai, United Arab Emirates		
Panama Canal, Panama		
Hoover Dam, Clark, Nevada		
Suez Canal, Egypt		
Palmanova Udine, Italy		
Indianapolis Motor Speedway, Indiana		

6 With a partner, write a paragraph about the possible impact on the Amazon forest of building highway BR163.

_____

_____

_____

_____

_____

_____

_____

_____

_____

_____

_____

Investigating Natural Geographic Features

Standards
Students know how landforms are created through a combination of constructive and destructive forces.

Google Earth Tools

- Toolbar: Placemark
- Status bar: Eye alt, elev*

Overview

Students will investigate natural geographic features, including landforms and ecosystems.

Vocabulary

- ecosystem
- erosion
- landform
- magma

Materials

- *An Elevated View* activity sheets (pages 64–66)

Procedure

1 Tell students that natural geographic features include landforms and ecosystems. Tell students that landforms are formed by natural processes, such as water and wind erosion that wear away the surface of the Earth, the collision of tectonic plates, and meteorite impacts. Also, explain that an ecosystem is a community of living things, such as animals, plants, and non-living things, such as water, soil, and air.

2 Distribute copies of the *An Elevated View* activity sheets (pages 64–66) to students and have them label the pictures of different landforms and/or ecosystems (question 1). Discuss any landforms or ecosystems that exist in your area.

4 Open Google Earth and **Fly to** Mount Kilimanjaro, Tanzania. **Zoom** to a view in which the mountain fills the **3D viewer** (an **Eye alt** of about 50 km or 30 mi.). Mount Kilimanjaro is a near-perfectly formed volcano that has eroded over time. Remind students that a volcano is a landform that is created when magma, or liquid rock under Earth's surface, rises to the surface of the planet.

* Tool introduced in this lesson

Investigating Natural Geographic Features *(cont.)*

Procedure *(cont.)*

 4 Point out the **elev** display in the **Status bar**. Tell students it stands for elevation, the height of a point on the surface of the Earth above sea level. Have students write a definition for elevation on their activity sheets (question 2). Hover the cursor over the top of the mountain and move it slowly down the slope to the bottom of the mountain and ask students to observe the **elev** display. On their activity sheets, have students write the highest and lowest **elevs** (question 3) and subtract to find the difference to determine the height of Mount Kilimanjaro (question 4).

 5 Center Mount Kilimanjaro in the the **3D viewer** and **zoom** out to an **Eye alt** of about 50 km (30 mi.). Point out the elevation of the snow and the treeline around the volcano where the vegetation ends. Measure the elevation of the treeline at several different points around the volcano. Ask students to describe on their activity sheets why they think the vegetation only grows to a certain elevation (question 5).

 6 Have students work with partners to find the natural geographic features listed on their activity sheets and complete the chart (question 6). Tell students to **Fly to** each feature and **zoom** to the specified **Eye alt**. Ask each pair to **placemark** the features and to use **elev** to find the highest and lowest elevations of each feature.

Extension Activities

- Island formation progresses from a sea mount to a lava-covered volcanic island to an eroded and vegetated volcanic island. Have students examine the Hawaiian Islands and try to determine which is the youngest island and which is the oldest island by looking at the natural geographic features.

- Have students investigate one landform, such as a peninsula, in different parts of the world. Ask students to look for commonalities and differences among terrain around the feature and write a descriptive paragraph about the common characteristics.

Investigating Natural Geographic Features *(cont.)*

Did You Know? ✕

Mount Kilimanjaro is the highest mountain in Africa and is formed of three distinct volcanic cones. The highest peak is dormant but could erupt again. Historically, the top of Mt. Kilimanjaro has been covered by an ice cap and glaciers. With increased global warming, nearly 80% of this ice has melted.

User Tip

In version 6.0 of Google Earth, the **Terrain** feature is on by default. In earlier versions of Google Earth, students will need to go to the **Layers panel**, under the **More layer**, and turn on the **Terrain layer**.

©2010 Google

elev display

Screenshots

Image ©2011 DigitalGlobe, ©2011 Cnes/Spot Image, Image ©2011 GeoEye

Mount Kilimanjaro, Tanzania

Name_____ Date _____

An Elevated View

 Label each landform and/or ecosystem with a term from the Word Bank.

Word Bank		
forest	grassland	river
glacier	lake	volcano

_____

_____

_____

_____

_____

_____

An Elevated View *(cont.)*

2 Define *elevation* in your own words: _____

_____

3 Use your cursor to find the highest elevation and the lowest elevation of Mount Kilimanjaro.

highest elevation: _____

lowest elevation: _____

4 Subtract the low elevation from the high elevation to determine the height of Mount Kilimanjaro. _____

5 Look at the treeline around Mount Kilamanjaro. Why do you think the vegetation only grows to a certain elevation? What factors might affect this?

_____

_____

_____

_____

_____

_____

_____

_____

_____

_____

_____

_____

_____

_____

_____

An Elevated View *(cont.)*

 Work with a partner to find the natural features listed below. Zoom to the specified Eye alt and write the highest and lowest elevations around each feature. Then, in the last column, describe the feature, including possible organisms in an ecosystem at the location.

Location	Eye alt	Highest elev	Lowest elev	Description of the Feature
Grand Canyon, Arizona	40 km (25 mi.)			
Dead Sea, Israel/Jordan	48 km (30 mi.)			
Mt. Everest, Nepal	35 km (21 mi.)			
Redwood National Park, California	1.6 km (5,500 ft.)			

Overlaying Abstract Geographic Features

Standard
Students know the purposes and distinguishing characteristics of different map projections, including distortion on flat-map projections.

Google Earth Tools

- Fly to box: lat/long*
- View: Grid*
- Status bar: Eye alt, lat/long*

Overview

Students will use Google Earth to investigate the abstract features of latitude and longitude.

Vocabulary

- abstract
- converge
- latitude
- longitude

Materials

- *Latitude and Longitude Lines* activity sheets (pages 70–72)
- markers or colored pencils

Procedure

 Tell students that abstract geographic features, like borders, the Equator, and lines of latitude and longitude, are visible on maps, but are not visible on Earth. Distribute copies of the *Latitude and Longitude Lines* activity sheets (pages 70–72) to students and open Google Earth.

 Fly to Africa and **zoom** to an **Eye alt** of about 9,500 km (6,000 mi.). Click on **View** in the **Menu Bar**, and then select **Grid** to turn on the latitude/longitude grid.

 Zoom out to a global view of Africa. The **Grid** includes bright yellow lines denoting the Equator, Tropic of Cancer, and Tropic of Capricorn. Explain to students that between the Tropic of Cancer and the Tropic of Capricorn, the sun shines directly overhead at least some of the year. Ask students to draw and label the Equator and the Tropics of Capricorn and Cancer on the globe on their activity sheets (question 1).

* Tool introduced in this lesson

Overlaying Abstract Geographic Features *(cont.)*

Procedure *(cont.)*

4 Tell students that latitude and longitude lines are useful for identifying regions on the globe. **Zoom** in to show students how the climate of Africa changes with latitude. On the globe on their activity sheets, have students identify and color the deserts, grasslands, and rainforests of Africa as they see them in Google Earth. Then, have students draw and label the latitude ranges that appear to get the most and the least amount of rain (question 2). Ask students to write what they can infer about rainy climates and the Equator from this information (question 3).

5 Rotate Earth to a view of the South Pole so that the Earth fills the **3D viewer**. Discuss the differences between latitude and longitude lines at the pole. Point out how the lines of latitude and longitude converge here.

6 Tell students that specific latitude and longitude points are also useful for finding locations that do not have names. Show students that the **lat/long**, or latitude and longitude, coordinates are always displayed in the **Status bar** at the bottom center of the **3D viewer**. To find a general area, only degrees of latitude and longitude are needed. To find a more specific place, you need to include degrees and minutes. Direct students

to the second page of their activity sheets (page 71) for directions on entering **lat/long** coordinates in Google Earth. Tell students that together you will use these directions to find a specific place in Google Earth.

7 To find the Hawaiian Islands, **fly to** 19 N 155 W and zoom to an **Eye alt** of 1,300 km (800 mi.). Turn on the **Borders and Labels layer**. On their activity sheets, have students write the name of this island chain and describe it (question 4).

8 To find a specific island, you need to include degrees and minutes. **Fly to** 19 49 N 155 28 W (**Eye alt** 250 km or 150 mi.) and have students write the name of the island and describe it (question 5).

9 To find an even more specific location, like the Mauna Kea Observatory, you need to include seconds. **Fly to** 19 49 34 N 155 28 27 W (**Eye alt** 6 km or 20,000 ft.). Turn on the **Places layer** and have students write the name of this place and describe it (question 6).

Overlaying Abstract Geographic Features *(cont.)*

Extension Activity

The Sahel in Africa is a latitude zone about 8 N to 18 N that has a rainy season between June and September, and a dry season between October and May. The land changes from a dry desert grassland to a lush green grassland. Images that show both seasons have been mosaicked at 13 3 48 N 5 0 57 E. **Fly to** this location. Tell students that the image on the right (with green vegetation) was taken in September. The brown image on the left was taken in January in the middle of the dry season. Ask students to write a paragraph about the challenges of living in the Sahel. Why do they think many animals migrate there?

Screenshot

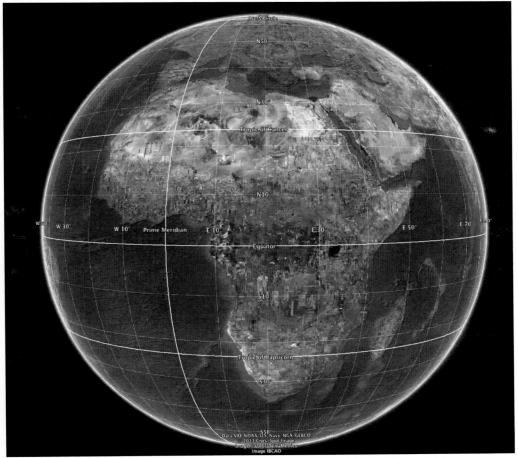

Grid view

Name_____ Date _____

Latitude and Longitude Lines

1   On the diagram below, draw and label the Equator, the Tropic of Cancer, and the Tropic of Capricorn.

2   Color Africa to show the deserts (tan) and the grasslands and rainforests (green) as you see them in Google Earth. Draw and label the latitude ranges that likely get the most and the least rain in Africa.

3   What can you infer about the relationship between rainy climates and the Equator?

_____

_____

_____

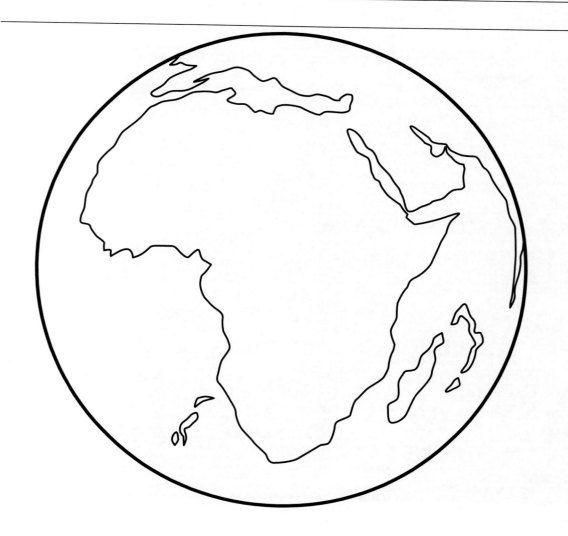

Latitude and Longitude Lines *(cont.)*

Entering Lat/Long Coordinates in Google Earth

Specific latitude and longitude (lat/long) points are useful for finding locations that do not have names. To find a general area, only degrees of latitude and longitude are needed. To find a more specific place, you need to include degrees and minutes.

The lat/long of the position of the cursor is displayed in the center of the Status bar, at the bottom of the 3D viewer. For placemarks, the latitude and longitude are displayed in the placemark window.

You can type lat/long coordinates in the Fly to box and Google Earth will navigate to that specific location.

Entering lat/long coordinates into the Fly to box can be tricky. It is not necessary to type in the symbols for degrees, minutes, or seconds—just type a space between each set of digits and letters (e.g., 31 17 47 S 174 3 53 E).

The easiest way to enter lat/long coordinates correctly is to have one person read the location aloud while another person types (e.g., "Thirty-one, space, seventeen, space, forty-seven, space, letter S, space, one hundred seventy-four, space, three, space, fifty-three, space, letter E.")

Use these directions to find the lat/long coordinates listed on the following page.

Latitude and Longitude Lines *(cont.)*

4 Fly to 19 N 155 W and zoom to an Eye alt of 1,300 km (800 mi.). Turn on the Borders and Labels layer. Where are you? Describe what you see.

_____

_____

_____

_____

5 Fly to 19 49 N 155 28 W and zoom to an Eye alt of 250 km (150 mi.). What is the name of the island? Describe what you see.

_____

_____

_____

_____

6 Fly to 19 49 34 N 155 28 27 W and zoom to an Eye alt of 6 km (20,000 ft.). Turn on the Places layer. What is this place? Describe what you see.

_____

_____

_____

_____

Constructing Reference Scales

Google Earth Tools

- Toolbar: Ruler*
- View: Scale Legend

Overview

Students will develop a reference scale that allows them to appreciate the size of features found in Google Earth.

Vocabulary

- reference
- scale

Materials

- *In Scale* activity sheets (pages 77–78)

Procedure

 1 Remind students of places they have already visited using Google Earth. Ask students if they think the Great Pyramid is bigger than their school or if their school is wider than the Nile.

 2 Explain that in Google Earth, using **zoom** does more than just let you see things closer or farther away—it changes the actual height of your eye above the surface, and therefore changes the scale of features. A famous structure can sometimes seem huge, but in reality it is not much bigger than your school. Other times, a landform like a crater or a lake may not seem very big, but your school or town could fit inside it.

 3 Distribute copies of the *In Scale* activity sheets (pages 77–78) to students and open Google Earth. Click **View** in the **Menu Bar** and select **Scale Legend**. A **Scale Legend** will appear in the lower left corner of the **3D viewer**. Show students the **Scale Legend** and tell them that it will give them a reference to estimate how large the things they see in Google Earth actually are.

* Tool introduced in this lesson

Constructing Reference Scales *(cont.)*

Procedure *(cont.)*

4 **Fly to** your school and **zoom** until the **Scale Legend** reads as close as possible to 100 m. Have students draw the outline of the largest building in their school in 100-meter scale on their activity sheets (question 1). Tell students that the drawing does not need to be detailed or exact as they are just trying to get a sense of scale. They will need to estimate the size of their school as compared to the **Scale Legend**. Is the school the same length as the **Scale Legend**? Twice its length? Half its length? Show how the hash marks on the **Scale Legend** can help them estimate.

5 Use the **ruler tool** to measure the length of the largest building in your school. Click once on the **ruler tool** in the **Toolbar** and a **Ruler window** will appear. Highlight the **Line tab** and then click on the pull-down menu to select meters for the length unit. Place the cursor over one end of the school building and click once and then click once on the opposite side of the building. The measurement will be displayed in the **Ruler window**. Ask students to write the length (rounded to the nearest meter) on the drawing of their school building (question 1).

6 **Zoom** out until the **Scale Legend** is as close as possible to 300 m. Ask students how the size of the school in the **3D viewer** has changed. Have them draw the school in 300-m scale on their activity sheets (question 1). Use the **ruler tool** to measure the length of the school building again and have students record the measurement on their drawings. Ask students if the measurement has changed significantly and why or why not.

7 **Fly to** the Great Pyramid of Giza and **zoom** until the **Scale Legend** is as close as possible to 100 m. Have students draw the pyramid in 100-m scale on their activity sheets in the box with their school building. Their drawings can overlap. Remind them to use the **Scale Legend** to help estimate the size of the pyramid. Use the **ruler tool** to measure the diagonal of the base of the pyramid and have students record the measurement on their drawing (question 1). Then, **zoom** out to 300-m scale and have students draw the pyramid again in 300-m scale.

Constructing Reference Scales *(cont.)*

Procedure *(cont.)*

8 Turn off the **Scale Legend** and **Fly to** Spiral Jetty, Utah. Ask students to guess how large this piece of earth art is in relation to their school. Turn the **Scale Legend** back on, set it to 100 m, and have students draw it on their activity sheets at 100-m scale (question 1). Use the **ruler tool** to measure the diameter of Spiral Jetty and have students record the measurement on their drawing. **Zoom** out until the **Scale Legend** reads 300 m and have students draw Spiral Jetty in 300-m scale.

9 Have students record the measurements of their school, the Great Pyramid, and Spiral Jetty in the chart on the second page of their activity sheets (question 2).

10 **Fly to** the remaining locations on the chart and view each in 100-m and 300-m scale. Measure the length of each and have students record the measurements in the chart on their activity sheets (question 3).

11 Have students determine whether each landmark is larger or smaller than their school (question 4) and then calculate the size difference between their school and each landmark. Have students record the differences in the chart on their activity sheets (question 5).

Extension Activity

Fly to each of the following locations and **zoom** until each one fills the **3D viewer**. Have students record the scale at which each place fills the **3D viewer**.

- Your school
- Rhode Island
- Montana
- The lower 48 United States
- China
- France
- Botswana

Did You Know?

Most of the units available to use in the **ruler tool** are well-known units, except perhaps the "smoot." This unit is a nonstandard unit of measure created as a prank by an MIT student and is equal to the height of that student, Oliver Smoot, at the time of the prank. See http://en.wikipedia.org/wiki/Smoot for more information.

Constructing Reference Scales *(cont.)*

Screenshots

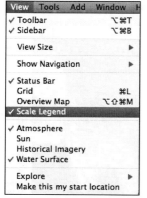

View: Scale Legend

User Tip

To alternate the **elev** and **Eye alt** displays between m/km and ft./mi., click **Google Earth** in the **Menu Bar** and select **Preferences** (Mac), or click **Tools** and select **Options** (PC). Under the **3D View tab** in the **Preferences window**, look for **Show Elevation** and select the units you want.

Spiral Jetty, Utah

Name_____ Date _____

In Scale

View each of the features below at both 100-m scale and 300-m scale in Google Earth and draw them in the appropriate boxes. Measure each feature in meters using the ruler tool in Google Earth and write the measurements on your drawings.

- Your school (measure the length of the largest school building)

- The Great Pyramid of Giza (measure diagonally)

- Spiral Jetty (measure the diameter)

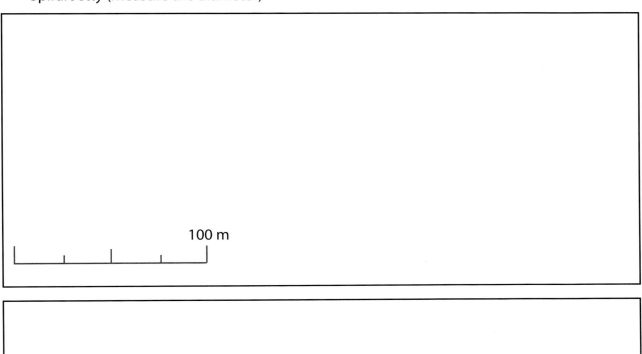

In Scale *(cont.)*

2 Record the measurements of your school, the Great Pyramid, and Spiral Jetty in the chart below.

3 Fly to the remaining locations in the chart below and view them at both 100-m and 300-m scales. Measure each landmark and write the measurements in the chart.

Location	Measurement (in meters)	Is it larger or smaller than your school?	How much larger or smaller?
Your school			
The Great Pyramid of Giza, Egypt			
Spiral Jetty, Utah			
The Coliseum, Rome, Italy			
Cadillac Ranch, Texas			
Stonehenge, England			
Angkor Wat, Cambodia			
Saint Basil's Cathedral, Moscow, Russia			

4 Compare the measurement of each landmark to the measurement of your school. In the third column of the chart, write whether the landmark is larger or smaller than your school.

5 Subtract to find how much larger or smaller each landmark is than your school and write the difference in the last column of the chart.

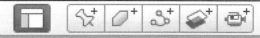

Sorting with Folders

Google Earth Tools

- Places panel: Folders

Overview

Students will begin to develop a series of folders to organize and categorize their placemarks. Students will add placemarks to these folders.

Vocabulary

- category

Materials

- *Sorting My World* activity sheets (pages 82–84)

Procedure

 Tell students that it is helpful to build a system to organize **placemarks**, not only to keep track of them, but also to see relationships between the **placemarks**. Distribute copies of the *Sorting My World* activity sheets (pages 82–84) to students and open Google Earth.

 Tell students that in this lesson you will demonstrate how to build an organized system of folders to keep track of **placemarks**, just like they would organize notebooks for school or files on a computer. Students will build their own folders after the demonstration. (***Note:*** One way to organize folders is suggested in this lesson, but there are many other ways to organize folders depending on your curriculum and classroom management.)

 Start by creating a main folder for the class. Right-click on the **My places** folder in the **Places panel**. Select **Add**, then select **Folder**. A **New Folder window** will appear that is similar to the **Placemark window**. Type *Our Class* in the **Name box** and click **OK**. (***Note:*** Alternatively, name the folder with the name of the class or the class period.)

* Tool introduced in this lesson

Sorting with Folders *(cont.)*

Procedure *(cont.)*

4 The new folder will appear at the bottom of the **Places panel**. Move it to the top of the **Places panel** just under **My Places** by dragging it with the cursor. This folder can hold all **placemarks** related directly to the class, such as the location of the school or places students have gone on field trips. Move these placemarks into the *Our Class* folder by clicking and holding a **placemark** with the cursor, then dragging it over the folder and releasing it.

5 Ask students to sort existing **placemarks** into categories on their activity sheets (question 1). Create new folders based on students' suggested categories.

6 To create more folders to hold **placemarks**, right-click the **My Places folder**, select **Add**, and then select **Folder**. Suggested folders include *Language Arts*, *Social Studies*, *Science*, and *Math*. Create these folders, or choose titles that are appropriate for your class.

7 Create at least two subfolders under each main folder for more organized sorting. For example, add subfolders titled *Family*, *Community*, or *Fieldtrips* to the *Our Class* folder. Add subfolders that include chapter names from the textbook, or literature selections sorted by author or reading level.

8 To add these subfolders, right-click on a main folder and select **Add**, and then **Folder**. Then click and drag to reorganize the existing **placemarks** into the appropriate folders for more specificity.

9 Continue to sort **placemarks** according to students' suggestions and have students list them in the appropriate locations on their activity sheets (question 2).

10 Ask students to think of other ways they could sort places. Have students work individually or with partners to to create **placemarks** and a folder system in Google Earth and write the folder and **placemark** names on their activity sheets (question 3).

Sorting with Folders *(cont.)*

Extension Activities

- Ask students to think of some **placemarks** that relate to their own lives that they might like to add to a personal folder. Have students create personal subfolders for books they have read, places they have visited, or class projects they have completed.

- Create more class folders to hold **placemarks** related to specific content or topics. Use a particular **placemark icon** or color to represent each category. Ask students to contribute **placemarks** relating to places or topics they would like to investigate.

Did You Know? ⊗

You can turn on all the **placemarks** at once to show the various connections between places that students learned about in class and places that make up their own lives, including cross-curricular connections. As students continue to "build their worlds," they will see the connections grow!

User Tip

If you can't find a saved **placemark**, search for it by clicking **Edit** in the **Menu Bar**, and selecting **Find**. In the **Find window**, type one or two words that identify the **placemark** and click either the up or down arrows to look above or below. The **placemark** will be highlighted (you may need to scroll to find it).

Screenshot

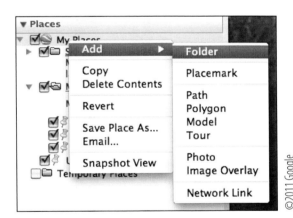

©2011 Google

Add folder

Name _____   Date _____

Sorting My World

 Go through the placemarks you created in Google Earth. Organize them by sorting them into categories, using the chart below. Label each column to describe the types of placemarks that are grouped there.

Category:	Category:	Category:
Placemarks	**Placemarks**	**Placemarks**

Sorting My World *(cont.)*

2   Label the diagram below to show the folder and subfolders your class created. Include the names of the placemarks in each folder.

Sorting My World *(cont.)*

3 Think of a way to sort your own placemarks. Create folders and sort placemarks in Google Earth and record your sorting system below.

Planning an Imaginary Trip

Standard
Students understand the characteristics and uses of maps, globes, and other geographic tools and technologies.

Google Earth Tools

- Layers panel: Borders and Labels
- Layers panel: Gallery: Travel and Tourism*
- Layers panel: More: Parks/Recreation Areas*
- Layers panel: Weather: Conditions and Forecasts*
- Toolbar: Placemark

Overview

Students will develop a deeper understanding of Earth by planning an imaginary trip that meets specific criteria for transportation, distance, and geography.

Vocabulary

- climate
- itinerary
- provision
- travelogue

Materials

- *Travel Time!* activity sheets (pages 88–90)

Procedure

 Distribute copies of the *Travel Time!* activity sheets (pages 88–90) to students and open Google Earth.

 Tell students they will use Google Earth to plan an imaginary trip to any place in the world. Use the following steps to model for students how to build their itineraries.

 Ask students to start planning by completing the checklist on their activity sheets (question 1).

 Tell students they must choose locations based on the criteria they have selected. For example, if a student chooses a tropical climate, would he or she find warmer temperatures closer to or farther from the Equator? On their activity sheets, have students list three possible locations that meet all their criteria and explain their reasoning (question 2). Then, select one students' choices to use as a model. **Fly to** one of their chosen locations in Google Earth.

* Tool introduced in this lesson

Planning an Imaginary Trip *(cont.)*

Procedure *(cont.)*

5 In the **Layers panel**, open the **Gallery layer** and turn on the **Travel and Tourism layer**. Turn on a few of the sublayers and look for **tourism icons** in the **3D viewer**. Click on the **tourism icons** as they appear to learn more about each tourist hotspot.

6 Open **More**, then open **Parks/Recreation Areas** and **Transportation** to see additional options for planning your trip. Turn on the layers you want to view and look for new icons in the **3D viewer**.

7 Investigate other layers such as the **Roads layer**, or the **Weather layer** for the **Conditions and Forecasts layer**. Use the **Borders and Labels** and **Places** layers to give accurate names to locations.

8 **Fly to** your own city as the starting point to begin planning the itinerary. Tell students they will complete their own itinerary on their activity sheets, listing at least three stops they could make on the way to their destination. Have them include bodies of water they will cross, and their preferred means of transportation (question 3).

9 As a class, **placemark** a model trip, including the stops. Save the **placemarks** in an *Our Trip* folder. Encourage students to choose views for each **placemark** that highlight the geography, climate, or landmarks.

10 On their activity sheets, have students list the kinds of provisions they need to pack for their trips (question 4).

11 Tell students to create an imaginary travelogue about their trips to describe what they saw, the climate they encountered, the type of geography they discovered, and any particular features or landmarks that were important. Have students use the travelogue template on their activity sheets to help them (question 5).

12 Have students present their travelogues to the class.

Planning an Imaginary Trip *(cont.)*

Extension Activities

- Give students restrictions to use inplanning their trips, such as they must travel in the Southern Hemisphere or they must travel part of the way by boat.

- Have students calculate the cost of their trip by researching airfares, train fares, or the cost of gasoline for car trips.

Did You Know?

Flight tracks can be plotted directly in Google Earth using the website http://flightwise.com/. Follow the links for flight tracking. Search by airline and flight number.

User Tip

As you investigate different layers, turn other layers off to avoid having Google Earth slowdown or crash.

Screenshots

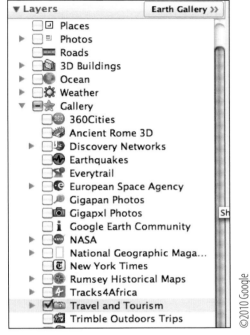

Travel and Tourism layer

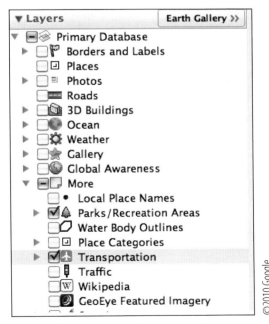

Parks/Recreation Areas and Transportation layers

Name_____ Date _____

Travel Time!

1 Place a check mark next to the ideal climate you would like to visit, the activities you would like to participate in, and the types of transportation you prefer.

Climate
- ☐ tropical   ☐ mild
- ☐ snowy   ☐ hot

Things to do
- ☐ swim   ☐ ski
- ☐ hike   ☐ visit museums
- ☐ visit relatives   ☐ go to sporting events
- ☐ go on a boat   ☐ try unusual food
- ☐ learn a new language   ☐ camp

Transportation
- ☐ car or bus   ☐ train
- ☐ plane   ☐ boat

2 List three possible locations for your imaginary trip that meet the criteria in your checklist. Explain how you chose these locations.

_____

_____

_____

_____

_____

_____

Travel Time! *(cont.)*

 3 Complete the itinerary below. Write the name of your starting point. List at least three stops you could make on the way to your destination. List any bodies of water you will cross and identify the types of transportation you will use.

Start: _____

End: _____

Three stops on my journey will be:

_____

_____

_____

I will cross the following bodies of water:

_____

_____

I will use the following means of transportation:

_____ (from_____ to _____)

_____ (from_____ to _____)

_____ (from_____ to _____)

4 Some provisions I will need on my trip include:

_____

_____

_____

_____

_____

_____

_____

Travel Time! *(cont.)*

5 On a separate sheet of paper, write a travelogue describing the journey you have planned. Use the following outline to help you.

On my journey, the climate of each location included: _____

_____

_____

On my journey, the geography was: _____

_____

_____

Some interesting features and landmarks I saw were: _____

_____

_____

My favorite part of the journey was: _____

_____

_____

Making Literature and Social Studies Connections

Standards
Students understand the forces of cooperation and conflict that shape the divisions of Earth's surface.

Google Earth Tools
- File: Save*
- Layers panel: Borders and Labels
- Places panel: Temporary Places
- Status bar: Eye alt
- Toolbar: Placemark
- .kmz file*

Overview
Students will continue to build and save their folders by developing Language Arts and Social Studies folders. In the process, students will investigate locations form literature that relate to historical events.

Vocabulary
- reservation
- wade

Materials
- *Islands of War* activity sheets (pages 94–96)
- *Code Talker: A Novel About the Navajo Marines of World War Two* (Bruchac 2005)

Procedure

 1 Tell students that there are many books with settings that they can find in Google Earth. Additionally, many of these books have settings that relate to historical events. Distribute copies of the *Islands of War* activity sheets (pages 94–96) to students and open Google Earth.

 2 Tell students they will investigate the setting of the book *Code Talker: A Novel About the Navajo Marines of World War Two* (Bruchac 2005). Create two new Google Earth folders: *Language Arts* and *Social Studies*.

 3 Ned Begay, the main character in this book, is a Navajo who enlists in the Marines to serve in World War II. Tell students that Ned lived on the Navajo reservation, located mostly in Arizona. Have them look at the map on their activity sheets.

 4 Turn on the **Borders and Labels layer** in the **Layers panel** and **Fly to** Chinle, Arizona, in the heart of the Navajo Reservation. **Placemark** Chinle and add it to a *Code Talker* subfolder in the *Language Arts* folder. **Zoom** in and investigate the landscape. Ask students to describe what they see on their activity sheets (question 1).

* Tool introduced in this lesson

Making Literature and Social Studies Connections *(cont.)*

Procedure *(cont.)*

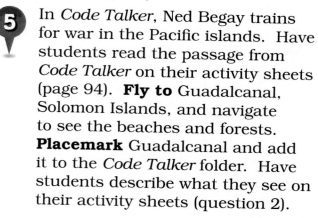

5 In *Code Talker*, Ned Begay trains for war in the Pacific islands. Have students read the passage from *Code Talker* on their activity sheets (page 94). **Fly to** Guadalcanal, Solomon Islands, and navigate to see the beaches and forests. **Placemark** Guadalcanal and add it to the *Code Talker* folder. Have students describe what they see on their activity sheets (question 2).

6 **Fly to** Bougainville Island, Papua New Guinea, and look at the beaches and forests there. **Placemark** Bougainville Island and add it to the *Code Talker* folder. Have students describe what they see on their activity sheets (question 3). Ask students if Guadalcanal was a good place to practice beach landings for Bougainville. Have students write their ideas on their activity sheets (question 4).

7 Ask students to compare Ned's home on the reservation in Arizona to the islands of the Pacific (question 5).

8 Tell students that in addition to being one of the settings of *Code Talker*, Guadalcanal was important during World War II. Return to Guadalcanal by double-clicking on the **placemark** in the *Code Talker* folder. **Zoom** out to an **Eye alt** of about 6,000 km (3,700 mi.) and center Guadalcanal in the

3D viewer. **Placemark** Japan and the west coast of the United States. Ask students to look at the location of Guadalcanal and Bougainville Island in relation to Japan and the United States. Ask students why these islands were important locations for the Allies to capture in the war against Japan (question 6).

9 Copy all the *Code Talker* **placemarks** in the *Language Arts* folder to the *Social Studies* folder. Point out to students that these **placemarks** pertain to both subject areas.

10 Show students the directions on their activity sheets for saving and transferring Google Earth data (page 96). Demonstrate to students how to save a **.kmz file**. Highlight the **placemark** or folder you want to save and click on **File** in the **Menu Bar**, select **Save** and then select **Save Place as...**. The file will be saved as a **.kmz file** on the desktop, or in another location you choose. Have students copy the *Code Talker* placemarks as **.kmz files** onto a memory stick or email them to transfer them to another computer. Once loaded onto another computer, they should double-click on the **.kmz file** to open it in Google Earth. The file will appear in the **Temporary Places folder** in the **Places panel**.

Making Literature and Social Studies Connections *(cont.)*

Extension Activities

- Ask students to consider other books to add to both the *Language Arts* folder and the *Social Studies* folder, such as *Anne Frank: The Diary of a Young Girl* (Frank 1953).

- Have students create multiple tier timelines to compare events in a story with events in history.

Did You Know? ✕

Placemarks and folders can also be emailed by clicking on the **Email tool** in the **Toolbar**.

Screenshot

Bougainville Island and Guadalcanal, Pacific Ocean

Name_____ Date _____

Islands of War

1 In *Code Talker* (Bruchac 2005), Ned Begay grows up on the Navajo reservation. Fly to Chinle, Arizona, and zoom in to explore the reservation. Describe what you see.

_____

_____

_____

_____

_____

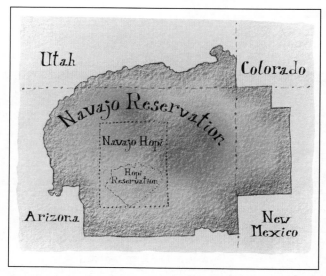

Directions: Read the passage below. Then answer the questions on the following page.

Excerpt from *Code Talker: A Novel About the Navajo Marines of World War Two* (Bruchac 2005)

"However, practicing a beach landing in a similar setting would help prepare everyone better than just going into a situation cold. So, where did we go to practice? Guadalcanal. From October 17 to 19 of 1943 we conducted landing exercises on the beaches of the Canal. Every Marine who'd be landing on Bougainville felt what it was like to wade through the surf up onto a boiling-hot sandy beach and then stare into the thick mysterious green of a steamy tropical jungle."

Islands of War *(cont.)*

2 Fly to Guadalcanal, Solomon Islands, and investigate the beaches described in the passage. Describe what you see.

_____

_____

3 Fly to Bougainville Island, Papua New Guinea, and investigate the beaches and forests. Describe what you see.

_____

_____

4 Do you think Guadalcanal was a good place to practice beach landings? Why or why not?

_____

_____

_____

_____

5 Compare Ned's home on the reservation in Arizona to the islands of the Pacific. How are they similar? How are they different?

_____

_____

_____

6 Look at the locations of Guadalcanal and Bougainville in Google Earth in relation to Japan and the United States. Why do you think these islands were important to the Allies in the war with Japan?

_____

_____

_____

Islands of War *(cont.)*

Sharing and Tranferring Files

You can save a folder, placemark, path, or tour as a .kmz file. Then, you can email the file or save it to a memory stick to transfer it to another computer and open it in Google Earth. Use the directions below to save the *Code Talker* **placemarks** and transfer them to another computer.

To save a file:

Highlight the folder, placemark, path, or tour in the Places panel. In the Google Earth Menu Bar, choose File, then Save, and then Save Place as…. The file will be saved as a .kmz file on your desktop (or in another location you choose).

To transfer a file to another computer:

You can copy a saved .kmz file onto a memory stick or email it to transfer it to another computer. Once on that computer, double-click on the .kmz file to open it in Google Earth, and it will appear in the Temporary Places folder in the Places panel.

To email a file directly from Google Earth:

Highlight the folder, placemark, path, or tour in the Places panel and click the Email button in the Toolbar. Choose Selected Placemark/Folder and click Email.

Sharing files:

You can also post a .kmz file to a website, blog, or social network so that others can download it and open it in Google Earth.

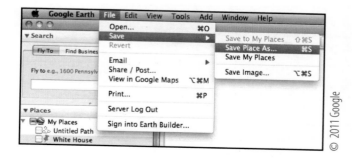

Connecting Science and Mathematics

Standards
Students know the locations of places, geographic features, and patterns in the environment. Students understand formulas for finding measures.

Google Earth Tools

- Fly to box: lat/long
- Status bar: Eye alt
- Toolbar: Clock*
- Toolbar: Placemark, Ruler

Overview

Students will use mathematics to investigate circular features on Earth.

Vocabulary

- aquifer
- impact crater
- pivot
- salt pan

Materials

- *Circles* activity sheets (pages 101–102)

Procedure

 1 Tell students they will explore circular features on Earth and investigate their connection to both science and mathematics. Distribute copies of the *Circles* activity sheets (pages 101–102) to students and open Google Earth.

 2 **Fly to** Edwards Air Force Base, Kern, California. **Zoom** out to an **Eye alt** of about 24 km (15 mi.) and look for Rogers Dry Lake. Tell students that the "lake" is a desert salt pan (it was once a lake) and is an important natural geographic feature for Edwards Air Force Base (AFB) that was used in the early Space Shuttle landings.

 3 **Fly to** 34 57 14 N 117 52 24 W. **Zoom** to an **Eye alt** of 3 km (10,000 ft.), and look for the world's largest compass rose. (***Note:*** If the compass rose is not visible, click the **clock tool** in the **Toolbar** and move the slider to the left until it appears.) **Placemark** the compass rose and save it to a *Space Science* folder.

 4 Create a new folder called *Geometry*. Right-click the compass rose **placemark** in the *Space Science* folder and select **Copy**. Right-click on the new *Geometry* folder and select **Paste**. The compass rose **placemark** will now appear in both folders, emphasizing cross-curricular connections.

* Tool introduced in this lesson

Connecting Science and Mathematics *(cont.)*

Procedure *(cont.)*

5 Use the **ruler tool** in the **Toolbar** to measure the radius of the compass rose in meters, and ask students to use the radius to calculate the diameter, circumference, and area of the circle (question 1).

6 Other prominent round features on Earth are impact craters, round holes in the ground caused by meteorites striking the Earth. Search for the impact craters listed in question 2 on students' activity sheets and **placemark** them. Measure the diameter of each impact crater in kilometers and ask students to write the diameters on the chart on their activity sheets and calculate the areas of the circles (question 2).

7 Have students use the chart to calculate the average area of these impact craters (question 3).

8 Save the **placemarks** in a new folder called *Earth Science*. You may also copy them into the *Geometry* folder.

9 Circular agricultural fields are prominent in Nebraska and surrounding states because irrigation water for these crops is taken from the Ogallala Aquifer under Nebraska. A center pivot system has a well in the center of the field that feeds a long sprinkler which pivots around the center to water the entire crop circle. **Fly to** Merna, Nebraska at an **Eye alt** of 50 km (30 mi.) and look for circular fields.

10 **Placemark** five different fields around Merna. Move these **placemarks** into the *Geometry* folder. Create a new folder called *Agricultural Science* and copy and paste the Merna **placemarks** to this folder.

11 Measure the diameters of the fields you **placemarked**. On their activity sheets, ask students to record each diameter and calculate the circumference of each circle (question 4). Then, have students find the average circumference of the given fields (question 5). Ask students to determine what the average field circumference indicates about the pivot system of irrigation (question 6).

Extension Activity

Placemark rectangles in Google Earth, such as crops, city boundaries, or buildings. Measure the rectangles and calculate the areas and save them in the *Geometry* folder. Create folders for these features, such as *Urban Planning* or *Engineering Feats*.

Connecting Science and Mathematics *(cont.)*

Did You Know? ✕

If you overlay the **Grid** onto the view of the compass rose on Rogers Dry Lake Bed (under **View** in the **Menu Bar**), you will notice that the lines do not match. This is because the compass rose is set to *magnetic* North and the **lat/long** lines are set to *true* North. The difference is called declination and is an important number for anyone using a compass because the difference is quite large.

User Tip

If you want to print an image from Google Earth, click the **Print tool** in the **Toolbar**. Select **Graphic of 3D View** and then **Screen**, **Low**, or **Medium**, depending on how high you would like the resolution of your print, then select **Print**. The dimensions listed next to the **Print** options depend on the size of the **Google Earth window** on your computer screen.

Screenshots

©2011 Google, Image U.S. Geological Survey

World's largest compass rose on Edwards Air Force Base, Calfornia

Connecting Science and Mathematics *(cont.)*

Screenshots *(cont.)*

Image ©2011 DigitalGlobe, Image ©2011 GeoEye, ©2011 Google, Image USDA Farm Service Agency

Pivot irrigation near Merna, Nebraska

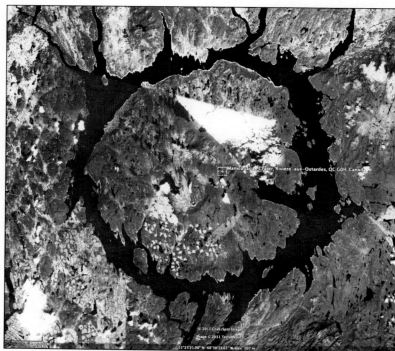

©2011 Cnes/Spot image, Image ©2011 TerraMetrics

Manicouagan Crater, Canada

Name_____ Date _____

Circles

1 Measure the radius of the compass rose at Edwards Air Force Base in Kern, California, in meters. Use the formulas below to calculate the diameter, circumference, and area of the circle.

Formulas
Diameter of a circle: $2r$ (where r is radius)
Circumference or a circle: πd (where d is diameter)
Area of a circle: πr^2 (where r is radius)

Radius = _____ m

Diameter = _____ m

Circumference = _____ m

Area = _____ m²

2 Fly to the locations listed in the chart below, and measure and record the diameter of each location in kilometers. Then, calculate the area of each crater. Round all answers to the nearest hundredth.

Location	Diameter of Crater	Radius	Area of Crater
Manicouagan Crater, Canada (Eye alt 130 km, or 80 mi.)			
Meteor Crater, Arizona (Eye alt 4.5 km or 15,000 ft.)			
Roter Kamm Crater, Namibia (Eye alt 4.5 km or 15,000 ft.)			
Wolf Creek Crater, Australia (Eye alt 2.4 km or 8,000 ft.)			

3 Based on the measurements from question 2, what is the average area of these impact craters?

_____

Circles *(cont.)*

4 Fly to Merna, Nebraska, and measure the diameters of five different circular fields. Record the diameters in the chart below. Then, calculate the circumference of each circle and record it in the chart.

Field	Diameter	Circumference
1		
2		
3		
4		
5		

5 Calculate the average circumference of the fields. _____

6 What does the average circumference indicate about the pivot system of irrigation?

_____

_____

_____

_____

Charting the Setting of a Book

Standards
Students understand how physical systems affect human systems. Students know the defining features and structural elements of a variety of literary genres.

Google Earth Tools
- Status bar: Eye alt
- Toolbar: Placemark: Description*
- Toolbar: Ruler

Overview
Students will learn that settings of books can be real locations that can be mapped using Google Earth as a means of further understanding a story.

Vocabulary
- shoal water
- trifle

Materials
- *On the River* activity sheets (pages 107–108)
- *The Adventures of Tom Sawyer* (Twain 2010/1876)

Tool introduced in this lesson

Procedure

 1 Introduce *The Adventures of Tom Sawyer* (Twain 2010/1876) by describing the setting of St. Petersburg—an imaginary small town along the Mississippi River. Twain modeled St. Petersburg after Hannibal, Missouri, where he lived when he was young. Tell students that while they cannot visit the imaginary St. Petersburg, they can visit Hannibal and see the town that inspired this story using Google Earth.

 2 Distribute copies of the *On the River* activity sheets (pages 107–108) to students and open Google Earth.

 3 **Fly to** Hannibal, Missouri. **Placemark** Hannibal and save it in a new folder called *The Adventures of Tom Sawyer*. Have students read Excerpt 1 on their activity sheets about the location of Jackson Island. Ask students in which direction from the town they should look to find the island based on the information in the excerpt. Have students answer question 1 on their activity sheets.

 4 Use the **ruler tool** to measure 6 km (4 mi.) south of Hannibal to find the island. **Placemark** the island (now called Fourmile Island) at an **Eye alt** of about 7.5 km (25,000 ft.) and name it *Jackson Island*. Save the **placemark** in *The Adventures of Tom Sawyer* folder.

Charting the Setting of a Book (cont.)

Procedure (cont.)

5 **Zoom** in and examine the island more closely. On their activity sheets, have students write a brief description of the natural geographic features of the island (question 2).

6 Reopen the Jackson Island **placemark window** by right-clicking on the **placemark** and selecting **Get Info** (Mac) or **Properties** (PC). The **Placemark window** includes a **Description tab**. Ask several students to share their descriptions from question 2 and type them in the **Description box**.

7 Tell students that in the book Tom and his friends met at midnight to head north of town to capture a log raft. Have students read Excerpt 2 on their activity sheets. Use the **ruler tool** to estimate the location of the raft and add a **placemark** to that location. (**Note:** Today there is a bridge across the river. Tell students that the bridge was not there when Twain wrote this book.)

8 Ask students why they think the boys chose a raft that was so far upstream from their island and not one that was just across the river. If students have trouble answering, ask them to consider the flow of the river. Have students write their answers on their activity sheets (question 3). Have several

students share their responses. Reopen the raft **placemark** and type some student responses in the **Description box**.

9 While on Jackson Island, Tom decides to sneak home to see his Aunt Polly. Have students read Excerpt 3 on their activity sheets. **Zoom** in on the island at an **Eye alt** of 800 m (2,700 ft.) to look for white ripples in the water that indicate the shoal water between the island and the Illinois shore. Ask students why Tom wades to the Illinois shore when his home is in Missouri. Have students write their ideas on their activity sheets (question 4).

10 Ask several students to share their responses. Add a **placemark** at the approximate location of the shoal water and type some student responses in the **Description box**.

11 Eventually, all the boys decide to go to their own funerals. Have students read Excerpt 4 on their activity sheets. **Placemark** the location where the boys came ashore and have students answer questions 5 and 6 on their activity sheets.

Charting the Setting of a Book *(cont.)*

Extension Activity

Mark Twain's sequel to *The Adventures of Tom Sawyer* is *The Adventures of Huckleberry Finn*, in which Huck goes on a journey down river on a raft and helps a slave named Jim escape to the north. Ask students how Huck could help Jim go north when the Mississippi flows south. If they headed south, where could they catch a steamboat to take them north?

Did You Know? ✕

The speed of the Mississippi River varies from 1.9 kilometers per hour (1.2 mph) at its headwaters in Lake Itasca, Minnesota, to 4.8 kilometers per hour (3 mph) in New Orleans where it empties into the Gulf of Mexico.

Screenshots

©2011 Google, ©2011 Europa Technologies, Image USDA Farm Service Agency, Image City of Hannibal

Fourmile Island

Charting the Setting of a Book (cont.)

Screenshots (cont.)

©2011 Google, ©2011 Europa Technologies, Image USDA Farm Service Agency, Image City of Hannibal

Two miles north of Fourmile Island

Name_____ Date _____

On the River

Directions: Read the passages below. Then answer the questions that follow.

> Excerpt 1 from *The Adventures of Tom Sawyer* (Twain 2010/1876) (Ch. 13)
>
> "Three miles below St. Petersburg, at a point where the Mississippi River was a trifle over a mile wide, there was a long, narrow, wooded island, with a shallow bar at the head of it, and this offered well as a rendezvous."

1 In which direction from the town should you look for the island?

_____

2 Find the island and placemark it. Write a brief description of the natural geographic features of the island.

_____

_____

_____

_____

> Excerpt 2 from *The Adventures of Tom Sawyer* (Twain 2010/1876) (Ch. 13)
>
> "They presently separated to meet at a lonely spot on the river-bank two miles above the village [Hannibal] at the favorite hour—which was midnight. There was a small log raft there which they meant to capture."

3 Placemark the spot where the boys met to capture the raft. Why do you think the boys chose a raft that was so far upstream from the island?

_____

_____

_____

_____

On the River (cont.)

Excerpt 3 from *The Adventures of Tom Sawyer* (Twain 2010/1876) (Ch. 15)

"A few minutes later Tom was in the shoal water of the bar wading towards the Illinois shore."

4 Placemark the shoal water. Why does Tom wade to the Illinois shore when his home is in Missouri?

_____

_____

Excerpt 4 from *The Adventures of Tom Sawyer* (Twain 2010/1876) (Ch. 18)

"They paddled over [from Jackson Island] to the Missouri shore on a log, at dusk on Saturday, landing five or six miles below the village…."

5 Placemark the location where Tom and his friends reached the Missouri shore. What are some of the natural features that would have made it easy for the boys to hide?

_____

_____

_____

6 Why is the river an important part of the setting of *The Adventures of Tom Sawyer*?

_____

_____

_____

Watching Events Unfold

Standards
Students know the ways in which changes in people's perceptions of environments have influenced human migration and settlement over time.
Students understand complex elements of plot development.

Google Earth Tools
- Layers panel: Borders and Labels
- Layers panel: Roads
- Toolbar: Path, Placemark

Overview
Students will follow a path taken by characters in a book and mark the path using Google Earth as a means of further understanding the setting of a story.

Vocabulary
- eclectic
- geyser

Materials
- *Walk Two Moons* activity sheets (pages 112–114)

Procedure

 1. Distribute copies of the *Walk Two Moons* activity sheets (pages 112–114) to students. Have students read the summary of the story *Walk Two Moons* (Creech 1994) on the first page of their activity sheets.

 2. In this story, Sal, the main character, moves from Bybanks, Kentucky, the home where she grew up, to Euclid, Ohio. Tell students that Bybanks does not actually exist. Sharon Creech modeled Bybanks after Quincy, Kentucky, where she lived.

 3. Open Google Earth and **Fly to** Euclid, Ohio, and Quincy, Kentucky, and **placemark** each city. Save the **placemarks** in a new folder called *Walk Two Moons*. Have students compare how the two towns are similar and different (question 1). Then, have students decide which city the quote in Excerpt 1 most likely describes (question 2).

 4. Have students read Excerpt 2, determine the location on Sal's trip that the excerpt describes, and use Google Earth to investigate and **placemark** the location (question 3). Save the **placemark** in the *Walk Two Moons* folder.

Watching Events Unfold *(cont.)*

Procedure *(cont.)*

5 Tell students they can follow Sal's journey from Euclid, Ohio, to Lewiston, Idaho, by drawing a **path** in Google Earth to illustrate the sequence of events. **Fly to** and **placemark** the locations listed in question 4 and have students add a description for each location in the **Description box**. Save the **placemarks** in the *Walk Two Moons* folder. Then, model for students how to create a **path** following Sal's route. Tell students that they will find detailed directions for creating and modifying **paths** on the third page of their activity sheets.

6 To model this path, turn on the **Borders and Labels layer** and the **Roads layer** in the **Layers panel**. **Zoom** out to a view that includes the **placemarks** at both Euclid, Ohio, and Elkhart, Indiana. Click on the **path tool** in the **Toolbar**. The cursor will turn into a square and a **Path window** will appear. Name the **path** *Walk Two Moons: Sal's Journey*. Do not close the **Path window**.

7 Place the cursor over the Euclid **placemark** and click to start the **path**. Move the cursor along the highway connecting Euclid to Elkhart and click several times as you head west until you get to Elkhart. Include about six points. Click **OK** in the **Path window** to end the path.

(***Note:*** When the **Path window** is open, you will need to navigate using the **navigation tools** to avoid placing unwanted points on the **path**.)

8 A *Walk Two Moons* **path** folder will appear in the **Places panel**. Move the **path** to the *Walk Two Moons* folder.

9 To continue the **path**, navigate to a view including the **placemarks** at Elkhart and Madison, Wisconsin. Open the **path** again by right-clicking on it and choosing **Get Info** (Mac) or **Properties** (PC). Click on the last point of the **path** to select it. You can now add new points to illustrate the journey through Illinois and into Wisconsin. Continue adding to the **path** and connecting the **placemarks** until you reach Lewiston, Idaho.

10 Click on the **Measurements tab** in the **Path window**. On their activity sheets, have students record the distance Sal and her grandparents traveled (question 5).

Watching Events Unfold *(cont.)*

Extension Activity

Create a **path** that illustrates Lewis and Clark's expedition. Distinguish Lewis and Clark's **path** from Sal's **path** by opening each **Path window** and clicking on the **Style, Color tab** and then in the **Color** box. Choose a color and a width for each line. Look at both **paths**. Where did Sal and Lewis and Clark's paths cross? Were these important points in each journey?

User Tip

When the **Path window** is open, navigate using the **navigation tools**. Using the cursor to navigate will alter your **path**. If you do this accidentally, you can erase the last point on a **path** by right-clicking (or control-clicking) on it.

Screenshot

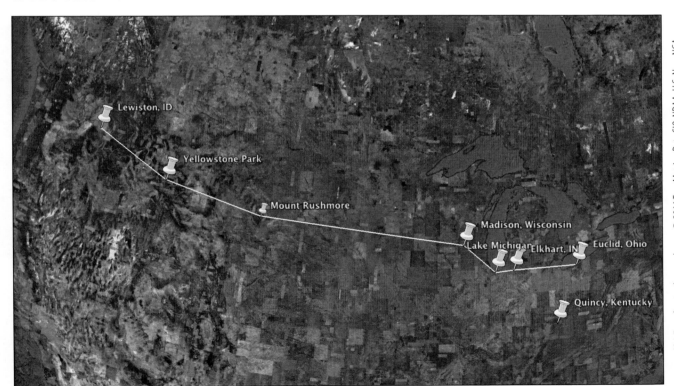

Path: Sal's journey in *Walk Two Moons*

Name_____ Date _____

Walk Two Moons

Directions: Read the summary of the story. Then answer the questions below.

> Summary of *Walk Two Moons* (Creech 1994) (School Library Journal 1994)
>
> Thirteen-year-old Salamanca Tree Hiddle's mother leaves home suddenly on a spiritual quest, vowing to return, but can't keep her promise. The girl and her father leave their farm in Kentucky and move to Ohio, where Sal meets Phoebe Winterbottom, also 13. While Sal accompanies her eccentric grandparents on a six-day drive to Idaho to retrace her mother's route, she entertains them with the tale of Phoebe, whose mother has also left home.

1 Fly to Quincy, Kentucky, and then to Euclid, Ohio. Write how the two towns are similar and different.

_____

_____

_____

_____

2 Read the excerpt from the story and answer the question that follows.

> Excerpt 1 from *Walk Two Moons* (Creech 1994) (School Library Journal 1994)
>
> "No trees?" I said. "This is where we're going to live?"

Which town do you think the character is describing, Quincy or Euclid? Why do you think so?

_____

_____

_____

Walk Two Moons *(cont.)*

 3 Read the excerpt from the story. Name the location that is described in the excerpt and then use Google Earth to investigate the location and answer the question.

Excerpt 2 from *Walk Two Moons* (Creech 1994) (School Library Journal 1994)

"Are we at the ocean?" Gram asked. "We're not supposed to be passing the ocean, are we?"

"You gooseberry, that's Lake Michigan."

"I sure would like to put my feet in that water," Gram said.

Gramps swerved across two lanes of traffic and onto the exit ramp, and faster than you could milk a cow we were standing barefoot in the cool water of Lake Michigan.

Location: _____

Why did Gram think they were at the ocean?

_____

_____

_____

_____

 4 Fly to and placemark the following stops on Sal's route to Idaho. In the Description box of each placemark, write about what happened there in the story.

- Elkhart, Indiana

- Madison, Wisconsin (Lake Mendota and Lake Monona)

- Mount Rushmore, South Dakota

- Yellowstone National Park, Wyoming

- Lewiston, Idaho

 5 Using the directions on the next page, create a path showing the entire route from Euclid, Ohio, to Lewiston, Idaho.

How far did Sal and her grandparents travel? _____

Walk Two Moons *(cont.)*

Creating and Modifying a Path

To create a path:

1. Click on the path tool in the Toolbar. You will see a path window and a square path cursor in the 3D viewer. Enter a name for the path in the path window. Keep the path window open. You can only modify a path when the path window is open.

2. Place the path cursor over the beginning of your desired path and click once. You will see a colored dot. Move the cursor to the next stop on your path and click again. A new colored dot will appear with a line between the two dots. Click on as many points as desired to complete your path. Click OK to close the path window.

When the path window is open, you will need to navigate using the navigation tools. Using the cursor to navigate will alter your path. If you do this accidentally, you can erase the last point on a path by right clicking (or control-clicking) on it.

3. A path folder will appear in the Places panel (or possibly in the Search panel) with the path icon just to its left.

To modify a path:

1. Right-click (or control-click) on the path in the 3D viewer or in the Places panel and select Get Info (Mac) or Properties (PC) to open the path window.

2. Change information as desired in the path window. You can modify the width and color of the path in the Style, Color tab.

3. Click and drag any point in the path to move it. To add points to the path, click once on a point to select it and then click anywhere away from the path to add a point after the selected point.

4. Click OK in the path window to save changes.

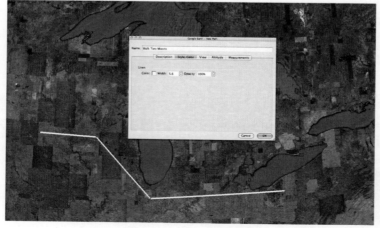

© 2011 Google

Touring a Book

Standards
Students understand the physical and human characteristics of place. Students use a variety of resource materials to gather information for research topics.

Google Earth Tools
- Layers panel: Borders and Labels
- Toolbar: Placemark, Tour*

Overview
Students will create a tour of the settings of a book as a means of summarizing a story and relating it to historical events.

Vocabulary
- chronologically

Materials
- *Living History* activity sheets (pages 118–120)
- sticky notes
- *Number the Stars* (Lowry 1989) or another reading book

Procedures

1. As students read *Number the Stars* (Lowry 1989), have them place sticky notes on pages involving important locations in the story.

2. To provide a dynamic view of a story's plot, students can make a **tour** of a setting. Distribute copies of the *Living History* activity sheets (pages 118–120) to students and open Google Earth.

3. **Fly to** Denmark, where the story takes place, and turn on the **Borders and Labels layer** in the **Layers panel**. **Zoom** out so that Denmark and Germany appear in the **3D viewer**.

4. Investigate the geographic features along the border between Denmark and Germany. Discuss whether it was difficult for Germany to invade Denmark. Have students answer question 1 on their activity sheets.

5. To help students begin to imagine the story, have them read the two excerpts on their activity sheets and then investigate and describe each location using Google Earth (question 2).

* Tool introduced in this lesson

Touring a Book *(cont.)*

Procedure *(cont.)*

6 Tell students that you will show them how to create a **tour** in Google Earth for *Number the Stars*.

7 Have students use the sequence map on their activity sheets to plan a **tour** of the locations from *Number the Stars* (question 3). Students should refer to their sticky notes to list important locations from the book in the boxes in chronological order. Suggested places include:
- Copenhagen, Denmark
- Copenhagen Harbor
- Amalienborg Palace, Copenhagen
- Trivoli Gardens, Copenhagen
- Klampenborg, Denmark
- Gilleleje, Denmark

8 Select the locations you will use for the model **tour**. **Placemark** the locations and save them in a *Number the Stars* folder. Arrange the **placemarks** in chronological order.

9 Click on the **tour tool** in the **Toolbar**. A **record-tour panel** will appear. The red button is the **start/stop button** and the **microphone button** is on the right (students will use the **microphone button** to add narration in the next lesson). The numbers indicate the duration of the **tour** in minutes and seconds (mm:ss).

10 Double-click on the first **placemark** to navigate to that location. To start recording a **tour**, click the **start/stop button** on the **record-tour panel**. The button will turn red as the **tour** starts to record. Wait a second and then double-click on the second **placemark** in the sequence. Google Earth will navigate to this **placemark**. Double-click the third **placemark** and Google Earth will navigate to this location. Continue in this way until you reach the last **placemark**. Then, click the **start/stop button** to stop recording.

11 A **play-tour panel** will appear in the lower left of the **3D viewer** and the **tour** will begin to play automatically. The **play-tour panel** includes (from the left) **go back**, **play/pause**, and **fast-forward buttons**, a **tour slider**, an indicator of the current time of the **tour**, a **repeat button**, and a **save button**.

12 Click the **save button** to save the **tour**. Give the **tour** a title in the **Name box** in the **Tour window**. Click **OK** to close the **Tour window**. Save the **tour** in the *Number the Stars* folder.

Touring a Book *(cont.)*

Procedure *(cont.)*

 13 Tell students they will find detailed directions for recording **tours** on the last page of their activity sheets. Have students create their own **tours** for books they have read and share their **tours** with the class. Remind students they can save their **tours** as **.kmz files**.

Extension Activity

Denmark is famous for other important accomplishments, including Viking expeditions, the development of renewable energy, and the manufacture of Legos. **Fly to** 57 4 36 N 9 54 43 E (**Eye alt** 500 ft) to see a Viking burial ground with stones arranged as ships that perhaps were set to allow Vikings to continue their journey after death. **Fly to** 55 41 14 N 12 40 11 E (**Eye alt** 3000 ft.) to find offshore windmills. **Fly to** Billund, Denmark, and search for Legoland. Have students extend their **tour** beyond the story in *Number the Stars* to include more of Denmark's accomplishments.

Screenshots

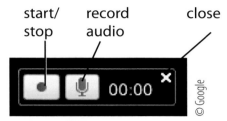

Record-tour panel

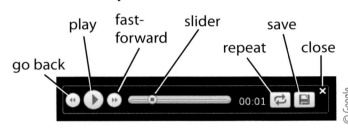

Play-tour panel

Did You Know?

To automatically record a **tour** of a series of **placemarks** organized in a folder, highlight the folder and click on the **Play Tour button** below the **Places panel**. To adjust the **tour** parameters, such as the time between **placemarks**, click **Google Earth** in the **Menu Bar**, select **Preference**, and adjust the settings under the **Touring tab**.

Name_____ Date _____

Living History

1 Look at Germany and Denmark in Google Earth. Do you think it was difficult for Germany to invade Denmark? Why or why not?

_____

_____

_____

2 Read the following excerpts from *Number the Stars*. Then, investigate the location from each excerpt using Google Earth. Write a description of each location in the charts below.

Excerpt 1 from *Number the Stars* (Lowry 1989)

"How the people of Denmark loved King Christian! He was not like fairy tale kings, who seemed to stand on balconies giving orders to subjects, or who sat on golden thrones demanding to be entertained and looking for suitable husbands for their daughters. King Christian was a real human being."

Location	Description
Amalienborg Palace, Copenhagen	

Excerpt 2 *Number the Stars* (Lowry 1989)

" 'See the land? Way across there? That's Sweden.'

'Maybe,' Annemarie suggested, 'standing over there are two girls just our age, looking across and saying, 'That's Denmark!' ' "

Location	Description
Gilleleje, Denmark	

Living History *(cont.)*

 Use the sequence map below to help you plan a tour of a book you have read that takes place in a real location.

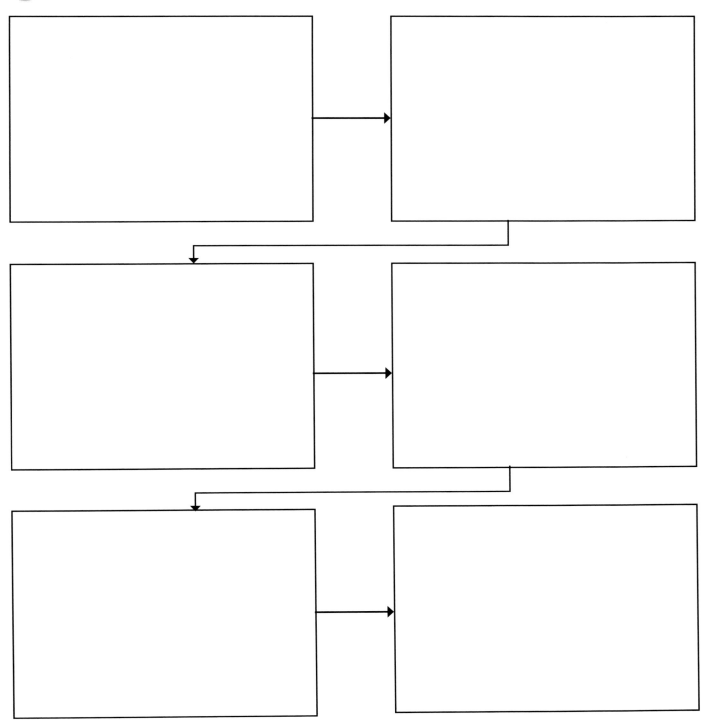

Living History *(cont.)*

Recording Tours

To record a tour:

1. Arrange your placemarks in sequential order in a folder. Double-click on the first placemark to navigate to the placemark in the 3D viewer.

2. Click on the tour tool in the Toolbar. A record-tour panel will appear in the lower-left corner of the 3D viewer. The red button on the left is the start/stop button. The numbers indicate the duration of the tour in minutes and seconds (mm:ss).

3. To start recording the tour, click the start/stop button. The button will turn red. Wait a second or two and then double-click on the second placemark. Google Earth will navigate to this placemark. Double-click the third placemark and Google Earth will then navigate to this location. Continue in this way to the last placemark. Then, click the start/stop button to stop the tour.

4. A play-tour panel will appear in the lower left of the 3D viewer and the tour will automatically start playing. The play-tour panel includes (from the left) go back, play/pause, and fast-forward buttons, a tour slider, an indicator of the current time of the tour, a repeat button, and a save button.

5. Click the save button to save your tour. Give your tour a title and then click OK.

Tour tool

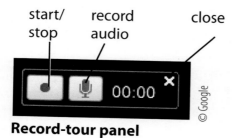

Record-tour panel

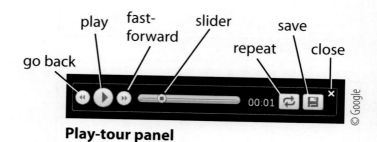

Play-tour panel

Creating a Book Report

Standards
Students know the ways in which changes in people's perceptions of environments have influenced human migration and settlement over time. Students make basic oral presentations to the class.

Google Earth Tools
- Toolbar: Placemark
- Toolbar: Tour: Audio*

Overview
Students will map the path of a book, create a tour of the locations, and add their voice to narrate the tour as a means of creating a book report.

Vocabulary
- narrate
- thematic

Materials
- *My Preview* activity sheets (pages 124–126)
- fiction or nonfiction book with real locations
- Google Earth tour (from the previous lesson)

Procedure

 1 Play some of the **tours** that students created in the previous lesson. Distribute copies of the *My Preview* activity sheets (pages 124–126) to students and open Google Earth.

 2 Divide the class into small groups or assign partners. Each group should choose a book that takes place in a real location. On their activity sheets, have students list the locations that they want to use as **placemarks** in their **tour** from the book of their choice (question 1).

 3 Have students choose three key **placemarks** that they want to describe in detail. Have students write brief descriptions of their three locations. Descriptions should include why the location is significant to the story and should highlight geographic features they see in Google Earth (question 2).

 4 To turn the **tour** into a book report, tell students they can add titles and voice narration to their **tour** in Google Earth.

* Tool introduced in this lesson

Creating a Book Report *(cont.)*

Procedure *(cont.)*

5 Have students create the **placemarks** they listed in question 1 and arrange them in order in a folder. The first **placemark** should show a regional view. Have students give this first **placemark** a name signaling that this **placemark** begins the tour. The name could simply be the title of the book. Advise them to choose large, colorful fonts for the **placemarks** using the **Style, Color tab** in the **Placemark window**.

6 For the last **placemark**, have students add a name to the **placemark**, such as *The End* that signals that the **tour** is over.

7 Have students add voice narration to serve as a summary of the book and tour. On their activity sheets, have students prepare a script of what they will say at each **placemark** as the **tour** records (question 3). Students should plan who is speaking and how they will transition from one **placemark** to the next during their **tours**.

8 Have students rehearse with partners before recording their narrations directly to their **tours**.

9 Tell students that to record their voices they should click on the **microphone button** in the **record-tour panel** and read aloud into their computer's microphone while recording their **tour**.

10 Have students record **tours** of the **placemarks** they chose in question 1. Students should time each other and try to keep their recordings under five minutes. Encourage students to take on the roles of the characters and to add some key details that reveal thematic elements of the story.

11 Tell students to use their descriptions to create a movie poster that gives a brief summary of the story (question 4). Students should draw at least one Google Earth view on the poster. Have students present their posters and play their **tours** for the rest of the class.

Extension Activity

Have students create a **tour** using the locations they discovered in the lesson on *Planning an Imaginary Trip* (pages 85–90). Tell them to use the **microphone button** to record a narrated travel diary.

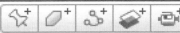

Creating a Book Report *(cont.)*

Did You Know? ✕

It is possible to add pictures and even embed video clips into a **tour**. However, doing so will significantly increase the file storage size of the tour and slow down Google Earth.

User Tip

You can stop a **tour** to look around by clicking on the **pause button** in the **play-tour panel** or by pressing the space bar.

Screenshots

microphone button

© Google

Record-tour panel

Image IBCAO, Image © 2011 DigitalGlobe, Data SIO, NOAA, U.S. Navy, NGA, GEBCO, Image © 2011 TerraMetrics

Name_____ Date _____

My Preview

1 Write the name of your book below and list the placemarks that you want to use for your tour.

Book: _____

Placemarks

1. _____

_____

2. _____

_____

3. _____

_____

4. _____

_____

5. _____

_____

6. _____

_____

My Preview *(cont.)*

2 Choose three significant locations and write a brief description of each. Your descriptions should include why the location is significant to the story, the time period, and any other details that are important.

Placemark	Description
1.	
2.	
3.	

3 Prepare a script of what you will say at each placemark as the tour is playing. Identify each speaker, and indicate how you will transition from one placemark to the next in your narration.

_____

_____

_____

_____

_____

_____

_____

_____

_____

_____

_____

_____

_____

My Preview *(cont.)*

 4 Design a movie poster to advertise your book tour. Include a catchy opening line and a brief summary of the story that includes the names of the main characters and the basic plot information. Draw at least one Google Earth view on the poster.

Experiencing the News

Google Earth Tools

- File: Save: Save Image*
- Layers Panel: Weather
- Toolbar: Clock

Overview

Students will use Google Earth to explore the effects of natural hazards or major world events on humans in different regions of the world and create a collage to memorialize the event.

Vocabulary

- breaches
- debris
- inauguration
- tsunami

Materials

- *Making Memories* activity sheets (pages 130–132)
- *TIME® for Kids* or another news source

* Tool introduced in this lesson

Procedure

Note: For several days before this lesson, have students bring in newspaper or Internet articles about current world events.

 Have students discuss world events that have been in the news recently. Highlight several important stories and identify the locations where these stories are taking place. Some events might include severe weather conditions, natural disasters or hazards, environmental accidents, new construction, or public demonstrations.

 Distribute copies of the *Making Memories* activity sheets (pages 130–132) to students and open Google Earth.

 Tell students that Google Earth has afforded us the opportunity to see recent images from major news events around the world. One example is an earthquake that occurred in Haiti on January 12, 2010. **Fly to** Port-au-Prince, Haiti, **placemark** it, and save it in a *Current Events* folder.

 Click on the **clock tool** in the **Toolbar**. A **timeline slider** will appear in the upper-left corner of the **3D viewer**. Tell students that each vertical line in the **timeline slider** represents an image that was taken of this area in the past.

Experiencing the News (cont.)

Procedure (cont.)

5 **Fly to** the Presidential Palace at **lat/long** 18 32 35 N 72 20 20 W, **Eye alt** 600 m (2,000 ft.). Move the **timeline slider** to August 25, 2009. On their activity sheets, have students describe the area (question 1).

6 Move the **timeline slider** to January 16, 2010. Ask students to look at debris from the earthquake. On their activity sheets, have students describe what they see (question 2). Have them look in all directions from the palace.

7 Move the **timeline slider** to the right to February 23, 2010. On their activity sheets, ask students to describe what they see in the park west of the Presidential Palace (question 3). Students should see blue and white tent cities, which were set up as temporary housing for people who lost their homes in the earthquake. Continue to move the **timeline slider** to the right. Ask students how long they think people lived in those temporary houses.

8 Close the **timeline slider** and turn on the **Weather layer** in the **Layers panel**. Ask students what the current temperature is at the Presidential Palace in Haiti. **Zoom** out and ask students to describe some of the weather they observe.

9 Tell students they will create a collage of Google Earth images. Direct them to the suggested events on their activity sheets on which to base their collages (question 4). Tell students they may choose one of the events listed or do research if they want to memorialize a different event.

10 Show students how to access Google Earth images for their collages by saving the images to the desktop. In the **Menu Bar**, select **File**, then **Save Image** and save the file in the desired location. Saved images can be imported into word processing or presentation software or printed out.

11 Have students use the planning template in question 5 on their activity sheets to plan which images they will save for their collage. Tell students to use three Google Earth images from the past in their collages to show changes over time. Students should include captions with each image, describing geographic features or landmarks that changed in Google Earth, the date the image was taken, and a Google Earth citation.

12 Students can add written descriptions or news articles to their collages. Have students display their collages and present them to the class.

Experiencing the News *(cont.)*

Extension Activity

Ask students to create a class news magazine called "Our Decade." Have students work with partners to find images related to news events from the past 10 years and write articles about the events focusing on geographic features that have changed due to these events. Compile the articles into a class magazine.

Screenshots

Presidential Palace, Port-Au-Prince, Haiti, August 25, 2009

Presidential Palace, Port-Au-Prince, Haiti, January 16, 2010

Name_____ Date _____

Making Memories

1 Fly to Port-au-Prince, Haiti, and use the clock tool to view the area around the Presidential Palace (lat/long 18 32 35 N 72 20 20 W) as it looked on August 25, 2009. Describe what you see.

_____

_____

_____

_____

2 Use the clock tool to view the Presidential Palace as it looked on January 16, 2010. Describe the appearance of the area on that day, including similarities to and differences from the August 25, 2009 image.

_____

_____

_____

_____

3 Describe what you see in the park west of the Presidential Palace in the image from February 23, 2010.

_____

_____

_____

_____

Making Memories *(cont.)*

 Investigate the events that occurred at the locations listed in the chart below. Choose one event (or one of your own choice) about which to create a collage. Use the clock tool in Google Earth to investigate how the area looked before, during, and after the event.

Location	Event	Date	Special instructions
Japan	Earthquake and tsunami	March 11, 2011	Look for the Fukushima Daiichi Nuclear Power Plant at lat/long 37 25 17 N 141 1 58 E
Outer Banks, North Carolina	Hurricane Irene	August 2011	Look for breaches in the roads
Joplin, Missouri	Tornado	May 22, 2011	Look for the brown streak between Highway 66 and East 32nd Street
St. Bernard Parish, Louisiana	Hurricane Katrina	August 29, 2005	lat/long 29 57 N 89 59 W at an Eye alt of 2.15 km (7,000 ft.)
The National Mall, Washington, DC	The inauguration of President Obama	January 20, 2009	Look at the size of the crowd that came to watch the inauguration.
Manhattan, New York City, New York	The World Trade Center	September 11, 2001	Look at the construction that has been completed in the years since the terrorist attack.
(Choose your own)			

Making Memories *(cont.)*

5 Use the template below to plan your collage about an important news event.

Event description: _____

_____

_____

Image 1

Location: _____

Geographic feature or landmark that changed: _____

Image date: _____

Caption: _____

_____

Image 2

Location: _____

Geographic feature or landmark that changed: _____

Image date: _____

Caption: _____

_____

Image 3

Location: _____

Geographic feature or landmark that changed: _____

Image date: _____

Caption: _____

_____

Tracking Pizarro

Standards
Students understand the characteristics and uses of spatial organization of Earth's surface. Students understand characteristics of the Spanish and Portuguese exploration and conquest of the Americas.

Google Earth Tools
- Layers: 3D Buildings
- Toolbar: Placemark, Ruler, Tour

Overview
Students will explore the geography along the path Pizarro took to conquer the Incas.

Vocabulary
- conquest
- conquistadores

Materials
- *Pizarro's Journey* activity sheets (pages 136–138)
- chart paper

Procedure

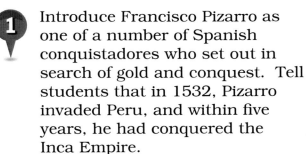

1 Introduce Francisco Pizarro as one of a number of Spanish conquistadores who set out in search of gold and conquest. Tell students that in 1532, Pizarro invaded Peru, and within five years, he had conquered the Inca Empire.

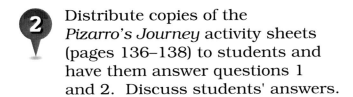

2 Distribute copies of the *Pizarro's Journey* activity sheets (pages 136–138) to students and have them answer questions 1 and 2. Discuss students' answers.

3 Open Google Earth. **Fly to** and **placemark** the locations in Pizarro's Log (shown in question 3 on students' activity sheets) and save them to a *Pizzaro* folder. Use the **Look joystick** and **zoom slider** to find views that highlight the natural geographic features of each location.

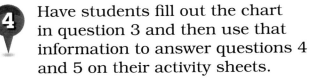

4 Have students fill out the chart in question 3 and then use that information to answer questions 4 and 5 on their activity sheets.

Tracking Pizarro (cont.)

Procedure (cont.)

5 **Fly to** Machu Picchu, Peru, the famous "lost city" of the Incas, and **placemark** it. Save the **placemark** in the *Pizarro* folder. **Zoom** in to investigate Machu Picchu. Use the **Look joystick** to find a view of the Andes that shows what the Incas may have encountered. Have students answer question 6 on their activity sheets.

6 **Fly to** Cuzco, Peru, and **placemark** it. **Zoom** out to a view that includes both the Cuzco and Machu Picchu **placemarks** (**Eye alt** about 170 km or 105 mi.). Use the **ruler tool** to determine the distance between Cuzco and Machu Picchu. Have students record this distance on their activity sheets (question 7).

7 Historians do not think the Spaniards actually found Machu Picchu. Use the **Look joystick** and **zoom** to navigate along the valleys between Cuzco and Machu Picchu. Ask students why they think Machu Picchu was so difficult to find (question 8).

8 Have students select three locations from Pizarro's Log and use the planning sheet to plan a **tour** (question 9). Then, have students use the **tour tool** to create a **tour** that highlights challenges of Pizarro's journey and the resources each location provided.

Extension Activity

Ask students to select another explorer and create a **tour** that follows the path of that explorer in Google Earth. Students should emphasize geographic features that were challenging to that explorer.

Did You Know? ⊗

As governor of the lands he conquered, Pizarro established the *Ciudad de los Reyes* (City of Kings) as his capital. This city was eventually renamed Lima, which became the capital of Peru.

Tracking Pizarro *(cont.)*

User Tips

Be sure to use **lat/long** 07 09 52 S 78 30 38 W when searching for Cajamarca, Peru, or else you will **Fly to** Cajamarca Region and not the city.

If your students have access to email, **placemarks**, **paths**, **tours**, and folders can be sent as **.kmz file** attachments. Highlight the **placemark**, **path**, **tour**, or folder you want to email, then click the **email tool** in the **Toolbar** and follow the directions.

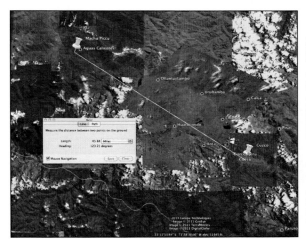

Distance from Machu Picchu to Cuzco

Screenshot

Machu Picchu, Peru

Name_____ Date _____

Pizarro's Journey

1 What are two characteristics of a safe geographical harbor for a ship? Why do you think so?

_____

_____

_____

2 What are two characteristics of a good place for a civilization to grow? Why do you think so?

_____

_____

_____

3 Using Google Earth, investigate the stops listed in Pizarro's Log, below. For each location, decide if the conditions described in the next three columns apply. Place an *X* in the column if the conditions described apply to that location.

Pizarro's Log

Location	A safe harbor	A good place to start a settlement	Provided resources (food, water, weapons, items for trade)
Isthmus of Panama, Colon, Panama (Eye alt 322 km or 200 mi.)			
Tumaco, Columbia			
Tumbes, Peru			
Paita, Peru			
Cajamarca, Peru (lat/long 07 09 52 S 78 30 38 W)			
Jauja, Peru			
Cuzco, Peru			
Lima, Peru			

Pizarro's Journey *(cont.)*

4 List two features that Tumbes and Juaja have in common.

_____

_____

5 Initially, Pizarro set up the Spanish capital in Jauja, Peru, but eventually moved it to Lima, Peru. Look at both locations in Google Earth. Why was the geography of Lima better than Jauja for trade?

_____

_____

_____

_____

6 Describe the geographic setting of Machu Picchu, including its elevation and vegetation.

_____

_____

_____

7 What is the distance between Cuzco and Machu Picchu?

_____

8 Use Google Earth to navigate along the valleys between Cuzco and Machu Picchu. Why do you think Machu Picchu was so difficult to find?

_____

_____

_____

_____

Pizarro's Journey *(cont.)*

9   Select three locations from Pizarro's Log. Create a tour that highlights these parts of Pizarro's journey. Use the planning sheet below to help you.

Location: _____

     Describe the location: _____

     _____

     Resources or challenges: _____

     _____

     _____

     _____

Location: _____

     Describe the location: _____

     _____

     Resources or challenges: _____

     _____

     _____

     _____

Location: _____

     Describe the location: _____

     _____

     Resources or challenges: _____

     _____

     _____

     _____

Mapping the Roman Empire

Standards
Students understand the physical and human characteristics of place.

Students understand influences on the economic and political framework of Roman society.

Google Earth Tools
- Layers panel: Gallery: Ancient Rome 3D*
- Layers panel: Gallery: Rumsey Historical Maps*
- Status bar: Eye alt

Overview
Students will use Google Earth to investigate daily life in ancient Rome and will work in groups to create a news report portraying life in the Roman Empire.

Vocabulary
- co-registered
- lede

Materials
- *Roman News* activity sheets (pages 142–144)
- chart paper

Procedure

1 Distribute copies of the *Roman News* activity sheets (pages 142–144) to students and open Google Earth.

2 Open the **Gallery layer** in the **Layers panel** and turn on the **Rumsey Historical Maps layer**. These are historical maps that have been scanned and co-registered, or matched, to the Google Earth globe.

3 **Fly to** Rome, Italy, and **zoom** in until two yellow **compass rose icons** appear (**Eye alt** about 7.5 km or 25,000 ft.). Click once on the **compass rose icon** labeled "Ancient Rome 1830" to see a **Compass Rose Map window** with a map, name, and date. Click once on the map in the window. The window will disappear and a **Rumsey Historical map** will appear in the **3D viewer** covering present-day Rome.

4 **Zoom** out to see the full extent of the **Rumsey Historical Map**, and then **zoom** in to an **Eye alt** of about 500 m (1,200 ft.).

Tool introduced in this lesson

Mapping the Roman Empire *(cont.)*

Procedure *(cont.)*

5 The "Ancient Rome 1830" **Rumsey Historical Map** is listed in the **Places panel** in the **Temporary Places folder.** Turn the map on and off to compare present-day Rome to Ancient Rome. (**Note:** The maps are not exactly co-registered, meaning that some locations on the Rumsey map are out of place.)

6 Use the **Places slider** located at the bottom of the **Places panel** to slowly make the **Rumsey Historical Map** more or less transparent. On their activity sheets, have students name some of the structures that still exist today, as well as some that no longer exist (questions 1 and 2).

7 Tell students that even though many structures of ancient Rome are gone, we can still see representations of the buildings. Open the **Gallery layer** in the **Layers panel** and turn on the **Ancient Rome 3D layer.** Zoom in until you see yellow **Ancient Rome 3D icons** that appear over the city. Hover your cursor over a few of the icons to see what places they represent.

8 Click on any **Ancient Rome 3D icon**, such as the "Theater of Pompey." An **Ancient Rome in 3D** window will appear, containing a small amount of information about that structure. At the bottom of the **Ancient Rome in 3D window**, click on **Ancient Terrain**. Wait for the layer to load.

9 In the **Ancient Rome in 3D window**, click on **Ancient Roman Buildings** (directly below **Ancient Terrain**). When you download this option, Google Earth will automatically **zoom** out and the layer will begin loading. (**Note:** This layer takes a long time to load.) This layer will allow students to view ancient Rome in 3D, similar to the **3D Buildings layer** or **Street View**. When the layer is finished loading, **zoom** back in and use the **navigation tools** to view the city. These constructed models allows students to "see" the city from the point of view of a Roman citizen.

10 Tell students they will be creating a fictional newspaper about Ancient Rome. Have students investigate the **Ancient Rome 3D** locations listed in the chart on their activity sheets and complete the chart (question 3). Then, have students identify two or more locations in each newspaper category to investigate in **Ancient Rome 3D**. Students will then choose one location from which to write a news report on a real or imaginary event from ancient Roman times.

Mapping the Roman Empire *(cont.)*

Procedure *(cont.)*

 11 Have students use the planning template on their activity sheets to build their newspaper report (question 4). Then, based on these templates, have students write their articles.

Screenshot

Extension Activity

Many Roman structures were dedicated to gods or leaders. Use **Ancient Roman Buildings** to investigate people in Roman mythology and politics.

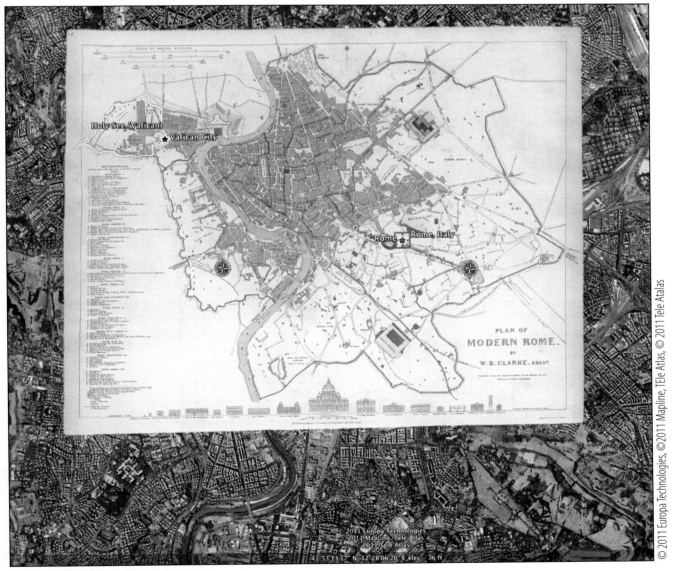

Rumsey Historical Map, Rome 1830

Name _____ Date _____

Roman News

1 Using the Rumsey Historical Maps layer, identify some ancient structures that still exist in Rome today.

_____

_____

_____

_____

_____

_____

_____

2 Using the Rumsey Historial Maps layer, identify some ancient structures that no longer exist in Rome.

_____

_____

_____

_____

_____

_____

_____

Roman News *(cont.)*

 Imagine you are a newpaper reporter looking for a story. Use the Google Earth Ancient Rome 3D layer to investigate each location in the chart below. Then, find two more places that fit in each category and investigate them in Ancient Rome 3D. For each category, briefly describe a real or imaginary event that may have happened at one of these places in ancient Roman times.

Newspaper Section	Locations	What may have happened here
News/Politics	• The Roman Forum • •	
Sports	• Circus Maximus • •	
Entertainment	• Colosseum • •	
Market/ Shopping	• Trajan's Market • •	

Roman News *(cont.)*

 Use the planning template below to construct your news article. Include the newspaper section in which your article will appear, as well as an idea for the lede, some key details that you will include, and some quotes from imaginary interviews.

ROMAN TIMES

Section: _____

Lede: _____

Details: _____

_____

_____

_____

_____

Quotes: _____

_____

_____

_____

_____

Going Back in Time

Standards
Students understand that culture and experience influence people's perceptions of places and regions. Students understand and know how to analyze chronological relationships and patterns.

Google Earth Tools
- Toolbar: Clock, Placemark
- Layers panel: Photos
- Layers panel: More: Wikipedia

Overview
Students will use Google Earth to discover relationships between social, economic, and political developments by observing Olympic stadiums and understanding the role of the Olympic games throughout history.

Vocabulary
- amenities
- stadium

Materials
- *The Olympic Games* activity sheets (pages 148–150)

Procedure

 1 Ask students to share what they know about the Olympic Games. Distribute copies of *The Olympic Games* activity sheets (pages 148–150) to students and open Google Earth. Tell students that they will learn more about the Olympic Games to help them fill in the blanks on the timeline on the first page of their activity sheets.

 2 Tell students that the first Olympics occurred in Olympia, Greece, in 776 B.C. **Fly to** Olympia, Greece (**lat/long** 37 38 17 N 21 37 50 E), to see the original stadium. Explore the area using the **Photos layer** and **Wikipedia layer**, **placemark** the stadium, and save it an *Olympics* folder. Look for a **photo icon** near the Statue of Zeus **Wikipedia icon** that shows an image of the site where the Olympic Flame was lit.

 3 Explain that the first modern Olympics took place in 1896 in Athens, Greece, in an ancient marble stadium updated for the occasion. Have students write "Athens, Greece" on their timelines for 1896 (queston 1). **Fly to** Panathinaiko Stadium, Athens, Greece, to see the stadium. Use the **Wikipedia layer** to learn more about the stadium and **placemark** it.

Going Back in Time (cont.)

Procedure (cont.)

4 **Fly to** Olympic Stadium, Athens, Greece. Tell students that this stadium and surrounding sports complex were built for the 2004 Olympics. Have them write "Athens, Greece" on the timeline for 2004. **Placemark** the sports complex. Have students use the **Wikipedia layer** to write a paragraph comparing the ancient Olympia stadium, Panathinaiko stadium, and the modern sports complex in Athens (question 2).

5 **Fly to** Olympiastadion, Berlin, Germany, the site of the 1936 Olympics. Have students add it to their timelines for 1936. **Placemark** the stadium and then click on the **clock tool** in the **Toolbar**. Move the **timeline slider** to 1953 to see the old stadium. (These aerial images were collected as part of WWII surveys.) Move the **timeline slider** forward in time to see how the stadium has been modified. In the chart on their activity sheets, have students write a description of how the stadium has changed (question 3).

6 **Fly to** the other Olympic venues listed on students' activity sheets. **Placemark** each location and use the **clock tool** and **timeline slider** to view the changes over time in each stadium. Have students add descriptions of how each stadium has changed (question 3) and add each city to the timeline.

7 Tell students that political events sometimes have an impact on the Games. There were three dates when the Olympics were cancelled: 1916, 1940, and 1944. Ask students to write "cancelled" on the timeline for these years and answer question 4 on their activity sheets.

8 Tell students that various countries have boycotted the Olympic Games over the years. Explain to students that there were two notable Olympic Games which were boycotted by multiple countries. The first boycott was in 1980 in Moscow, Russia. **Fly to** Olimpiyskiy, Kiev, Russia, to see the stadium. The next Olympic Games that were boycotted were held in 1984 in Los Angeles, California. **Fly to** Los Angeles Memorial Coliseum, Los Angeles, California, to see the stadium. Have students add the names of these cities and "boycott" to their timelines for these years and answer question 5.

9 Have students use the timeline to sort the summer Olympic host cities by continent and answer question 6 on their activity sheets.

Going Back in Time *(cont.)*

Extension Activity

Have students investigate other former Olympic venues. Have them determine the elevation of each stadium and write an essay discussing how the elevation of different stadiums might impact the outcome of the Olympic events.

Did You Know? ✕

London is the first city to host the Olympic games three times: 1908, 1948, and 2012.

Screenshot

Olympia, Greece

Name_____   Date _____

The Olympic Games *(cont.)*

 Use the timeline of the modern Olympic Games below to answer the questions on the following pages. You will fill in the blanks as you work through the lesson.

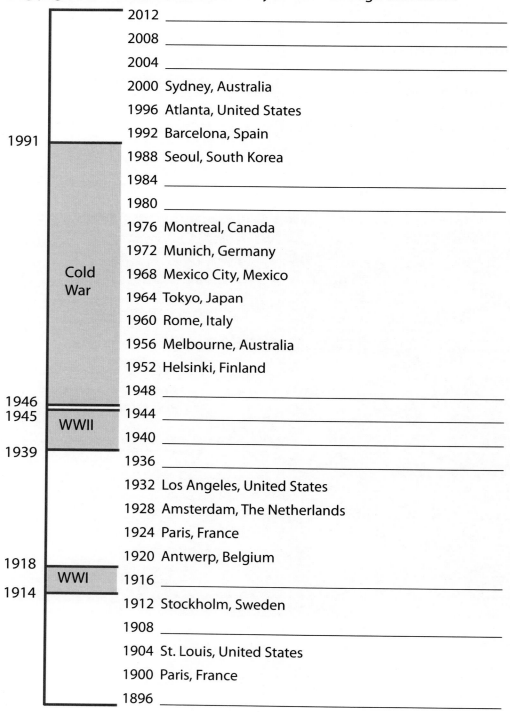

```
                    2012  _____
                    2008  _____
                    2004  _____
                    2000  Sydney, Australia
                    1996  Atlanta, United States
                    1992  Barcelona, Spain
    1991            1988  Seoul, South Korea
                    1984  _____
                    1980  _____
                    1976  Montreal, Canada
                    1972  Munich, Germany
            Cold    1968  Mexico City, Mexico
            War     1964  Tokyo, Japan
                    1960  Rome, Italy
                    1956  Melbourne, Australia
                    1952  Helsinki, Finland
                    1948  _____
    1946
    1945    WWII    1944  _____
                    1940  _____
    1939
                    1936  _____
                    1932  Los Angeles, United States
                    1928  Amsterdam, The Netherlands
                    1924  Paris, France
    1918            1920  Antwerp, Belgium
            WWI     1916  _____
    1914
                    1912  Stockholm, Sweden
                    1908  _____
                    1904  St. Louis, United States
                    1900  Paris, France
                    1896  _____
```

Name_____ Date _____

The Olympic Games *(cont.)*

2 Using the Wikipedia layer to investigate and write a paragraph comparing the ancient Olympia stadium, the Panathinaiko Stadium in Athens, and the modern Olympic Stadium and sports complex in Athens.

_____

_____

_____

_____

_____

_____

_____

_____

3 Fly to the Olympic venues listed in the chart below. Use the clock tool view current and past images of each stadium. Describe the changes you see at each location.

Venue and City	Host Year(s)	Description of Change
Olympiastadion, Berlin, Germany	1936	
Beijing National Stadium, Beijing, China	2008	
Olympic Stadium, London, England 51 32 18 N 0 00 59 W	1908, 1948, 2012	

The Olympic Games *(cont.)*

4 The Olympics were cancelled in 1916, 1940, and 1944. What else was happening in the world during those times that caused the Games to be cancelled, based on the information in the timeline?

_____

Do you think the Olympics should have been cancelled? Why or why not?

_____

_____

_____

_____

5 Using the information in the timeline, identify the political struggle going on in the world that contributed to the boycotts of the 1980 Moscow Olympic Games and the 1984 Los Angeles Olympic Games.

_____

6 Use the timeline to determine how many times each continent has hosted the Summer Olympic Games.

Europe: _____

Asia:_____

Africa: _____

Australia: _____

North America: _____

South America: _____

Why do you think certain continents have hosted more Olympic Games than others?

_____

_____

_____

_____

_____

_____

Inspecting Icy Climates

Standards
Students know the causes and effects of changes in a place over time. Students know features that can impact Earth's climate.

Google Earth Tools
- Earth Gallery: Arctic Sea Ice*

Overview
Students will use NASA data provided to Google Earth to study ice and learn how changes in glaciers and sea ice help us monitor climate change.

Vocabulary
- accumulate
- advance
- glacier
- iceberg
- ice sheet
- moraine
- retreat
- sea ice

Materials
- *Glaciers and Sea Ice* activity sheets (pages 155–156)
- markers or colored pencils

Procedure

 1 Remind students that 0°C (32°F) is the temperature at which liquid water freezes into ice, or ice melts back into liquid water. On Earth, this transition between two states of water dominates the climate in the polar regions. Distribute copies of the *Glaciers and Sea Ice* activity sheets (pages 155–156) to students and open Google Earth.

 2 Explain to students that ice appears on Earth in several forms. It may initially arrive as snow, which accumulates into glaciers in cold regions. If more snow accumulates on a glacier than melts, glaciers advance, or grow larger. If more melting occurs than snow accumulation, the glacier retreats, or shrinks. When glaciers retreat, it indicates that the climate is warming.

 3 **Fly to** the three glaciers listed on the activity sheet and navigate around the glaciers (question 1). Ask students to write a description of each glacier in the third column of the chart. **Placemark** the glaciers and add them to a *Glaciers* folder. Then, have students write two characteristics that would help them recognize other glaciers around the world (question 2).

* Tool introduced in this lesson

Inspecting Icy Climates *(cont.)*

Procedure *(cont.)*

4 If glaciers grow to a size that covers an entire land mass, like Antarctica or Greenland, they are called ice sheets. Navigate the coastlines of Antarctica or Greenland and ask students to describe what the edges of ice sheets look like (question 3).

5 When glaciers reach the ocean before the temperature rises above 0°C (32°F), the glaciers break off into the ocean and form icebergs. **Fly to** 62 52 21 N 42 25 1 W, Eye alt 35 km (20 mi.), and ask students to identify the icebergs coming off the glacier.

6 As glaciers advance, they push mounds of dirt in front of and beside them. When they retreat, these mounds of dirt, called moraines, are left behind. Show students the arcing ripples of dirt to the south of Malaspina Glacier, Alaska (59 55 44 N 140 32 32 W, **Eye alt** 80 km or 50 mi.).

7 Ask students to list two characteristics of icebergs and moraines that would help them recognize these features in other parts of the world (question 4).

8 Ice can also form from ocean water if ocean and air temperatures are cold enough. Ice floats on the ocean surface because ice is less dense than water (just as ice cubes float in a glass of water).

9 To see the sea ice, open the **Earth Gallery** at the top of the **Layers panel**. Using the search box, search for "Arctic Sea Ice." Under *Arctic Sea Ice, The National Snow and Ice Data Center*, click *Open in Google Earth*. In the **3D viewer** you will see an **icon** labeled *Arctic Sea Ice Extent*. Click on the icon and a pop-up window will appear. Click on **Download & View the Layer**.

10 In the **Temporary Places folder** in the **Places panel**, the **NSCID Climate Change layer** is automatically turned on. Turn off the entire **NSCID Climate Change layer** to eliminate unnecessary logos. Then, open **September 1979–2008** and open the **Data layer**. Turn on the first layer in **Data**, the **197909 layer**, which shows the sea ice from September 1979. On their activity sheets, have students shade the extent of the ice on the map in yellow (question 5).

11 Turn off the **197909 layer** and turn on the **200809 layer** (the last layer). This shows the sea ice from September 2008. Ask students to shade the extent of the ice in red on the map on their activity sheets (question 6).

Inspecting Icy Climates *(cont.)*

Procedure *(cont.)*

 12 Ask students to estimate the percent of change in the sea ice (question 7).

 13 Turn on the entire **Data layer** so that all the sea ice layers are displayed, one on top of the other, in the **3D viewer**. On the **timeline slider**, slide the right slider all the way to the right and the left slider all the way to the left. Click the **play button** (it looks like a clock with an arrow on it) and each layer will disappear in turn, animating the shrinking of the Arctic sea ice.

 14 Apart from looking for moraines and glacial lakes that indicate a glacier is retreating, scientists compare past and present photographs of glaciers to see if they have changed. **Fly to** 59 53 26 N 150 01 25 W (**Eye alt** 80 km or 50 mi.) and click on the **Arctic Sea Ice icons** to open pop-up windows with photographs. Click on the years under each pair of photographs to see how that glacier has changed over time. On their activity sheets, ask students to describe the changes that they see (question 8).

Extension Activity

Glaciers form at high elevations like on Mount Everest, Nepal and the mountains around Chamonix, France. Have students look for evidence that shows these glaciers are retreating by identifying moraines and glacial ponds.

Screenshots

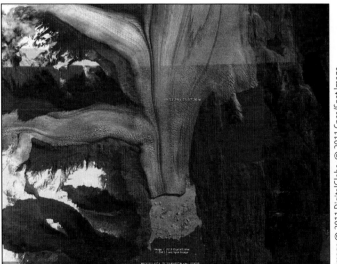

Image © 2011 DigitalGlobe, © 2011 Cnes/Spot Image

Glacier at border of Argentina and Chile

Inspecting Icy Climates *(cont.)*

Screenshots *(cont.)*

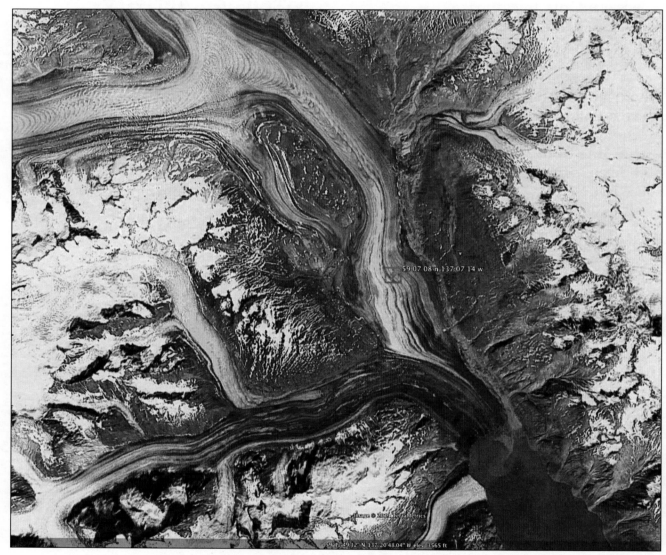

Glacier at border of Alaska and Canada

Name_____ Date _____

Glaciers and Sea Ice

Directions: Fly to the three glaciers listed below and zoom in to get a closer look. Describe what you see in the third column. Then, answer the questions below.

Glacier	Location	Description
Alaska	59 07 08 N 137 07 14 W Eye alt 15 km (10 mi.)	
Argentine/Chile border	49 53 29 S 73 17 26 W Eye alt 24 km (15 mi.)	
Fox Glacier, New Zealand	43 30 13 S 170 05 42 E Eye alt 24 km (15 mi.)	

2 Write two common characteristics of a glacier that would help you recognize other glaciers around the world.

_____

_____

3 Navigate around the coastlines of Antarctica or Greenland. Describe what the edges of ice sheets look like.

_____

_____

4 Investigate Malaspina Glacier, Alaska. List two characteristics of icebergs and moraines that would help you recognize them in other parts of the world.

icebergs: _____

_____

moraines: _____

_____

Glaciers and Sea Ice *(cont.)*

Directions: Use the map below to answer questions 5 through 7.

5 Use Google Earth to look at the data on sea ice from 1979. Shade the the extent of the ice on the map in yellow.

6 Look at the data on sea ice from 2008. Shade the extent of the ice on the map in red.

7 Estimate the percent of change in the sea ice.

_____

8 Look at past photographs of glaciers to see if they have changed. Fly to 59 53 26 N 150 01 25 W (Eye alt 80 km or 50 mi.) and look for the Arctic Sea Ice icons. Click on each one to see photographs of how that glacier has changed over time. Describe the changes that you see.

_____

_____

_____

_____

_____

_____

_____

_____

Colliding Plates

Standards

Students know how landforms are created through a combination of constructive and destructive forces. Students know that the Earth's crust is divided into plates that move at extremely slow rates in response to movements in the mantle.

Google Earth Tools

- Layers panel: Borders and Labels
- Layers panel: Gallery: Earthquakes, Volcanoes*

Overview

Students will investigate plate tectonics and will discover how volcanoes and earthquakes relate to plate boundaries.

Vocabulary

- convergent
- divergent
- tectonics
- transform

Materials

- *Volcanoes* activity sheets (pages 160–162)
- modeling clay or dough in different colors

Procedure

 Tell students that scientists describe the boundaries of Earth's tectonic plates in three ways: convergent, divergent, and transform. Distribute copies of the *Volcanoes* activity sheets (pages 160–162) to students and open Google Earth. Turn on the **Borders and Labels layer**.

 On their activity sheets, have students read the definitions of each type of plate boundary. Have them use two pieces of modeling clay or dough in different colors to represent the movement of each type of boundary. Having done this, ask them to predict what kind of landform they would expect to find along each type of boundary (question 1).

 Open the **Gallery layer** in the **Layers panel** and turn on the **Earthquakes layer** and the **Volcanoes layer**. Navigate to Washington and Oregon in the northwestern United States at an **Eye alt** of 1,300 km (800 mi.). Tell students the volcanic mountains that run north to south across Oregon and Washington are called the Cascade Range. **Placemark** the area and add it to a *Volcanoes* folder.

* Tool introduced in this lesson

Colliding Plates *(cont.)*

Procedure *(cont.)*

4 Have students choose a color and shade the area of the Cascade Range on the plate boundary map on their activity sheets and identify which of the three types of boundaries they think exists here (question 2).

5 **Fly to** Tokyo, Japan, at an **Eye alt** of about 1,500 km (950 mi.). Have students choose a second color and shade the area of volcanoes and earthquakes on their maps and identify which type of boundary exists here (question 3).

6 **Fly to** Point Reyes, California, at an **Eye alt** of about 64 km (40 mi.) to view part of the San Andreas Fault. Have students shade the fault on their maps and identify the type of boundary they think exists here (question 4).

7 Have students write a paragraph describing the relationship between plate tectonics, volcanoes, earthquakes, and other landforms on Earth (question 5).

Extension Activity

Have students discover the evolution of the continental boundaries in Google Earth. Look in the top right corner of the **Layers panel** for a button called **Earth Gallery**. Click on it and search for **Global Paleogeographic Views** under the **Ocean tab**. Open it in Google Earth and use the **timeline slider** at the top left corner of the **3D viewer** to go back in time 4,600 million years ago. Then slowly move the slider from left to right to witness the changing shapes of the continents. Have students create timelines and describe each era in terms of climate and continental locations on Earth.

Colliding Plates *(cont.)*

User Tip

If you have an older version of Google Earth (before 6.0), the **Gallery** may be found under the **Add Content button** in the **Places panel**.

Did You Know?

The first period represented in the **Global Paleogeographic Views** is the Precambrian period, 4,600 million years ago. This period represents 88% of geologic time!

Screenshot

Cascade volcanoes in Washington and Oregon

Name_____ Date _____

Volcanoes

1 Read the definitions of three different types of tectonic plate boundaries below. Use two pieces of modeling clay or dough in different colors to represent tectonic plates. Move the pieces together as described below to model each type of boundary. Describe what happens to the clay in your own words on the lines below.

- **Convergent boundaries** exist where two plates crash into one other and one plate is subducted below the other, thrusting the top plate upward.

_____

_____

_____

What landform might be created by this type of boundary?

_____

- **Divergent boundaries** exist where two plates move away from one another. Molten lava often rises to the surface and escapes through the gaps.

_____

_____

_____

What landform might be created by this type of boundary?

_____

- **Transform boundaries** exist where two plates slide past each other horizontally.

_____

_____

_____

What landform might be created by this type of boundary?

_____

Volcanoes *(cont.)*

Directions: Use the plate boundary map below to answer the questions on the following page.

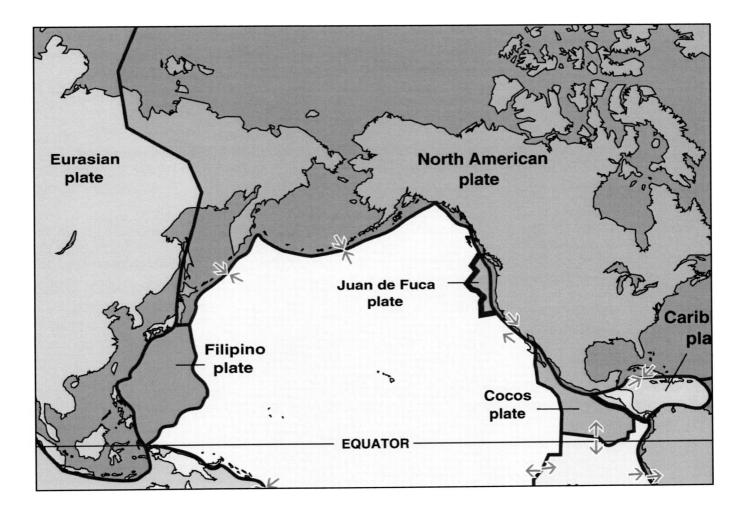

Volcanoes *(cont.)*

2 Turn on the Volcanoes and Earthquakes layers and Fly to the Cascade Range in Oregon and Washington. Choose a color and shade the area on the map where the Cascade volcanoes are located. What kind of plate boundary do you think exists here?

_____

3 Fly to Tokyo, Japan. Choose a new color and shade the area of volcanoes and earthquakes around Tokyo on the map. What kind of plate boundary do you think exists here?

_____

4 Fly to Point Reyes, California and observe the San Andreas fault. Choose a third color and shade the area of earthquakes along the Mid-Atlantic Ridge and the San Andreas Fault. What kind of plate boundary do you think exists here?

_____

5 On a separate piece of paper, write a paragraph describing the relationship between plate tectonics, earthquakes, volcanoes, and other landforms on Earth.

Shading the Earth

Standards
Students understand concepts such as axis, seasons, rotation, and revolution (Earth-Sun relations). Students know how the tilt of the Earth's axis and the Earth's revolution around the Sun affect seasons and weather patterns.

Google Earth Tools
- Status bar: Eye alt
- Toolbar: Sun*
- View: Grid

Overview
Students will study the patterns of the sun and Earth and how the rotation of Earth relates to a day and a year at different latitudes. Students will see how these patterns may have affected early polar explorers.

Vocabulary
- axis
- Greenwich Mean Time (GMT)
- revolve
- rotate

Materials
- *As the World Turns* activity sheets (pages 166–168)

Procedure

1 Distribute copies of the *As the World Turns* activity sheets (pages 166–168) to students and open Google Earth.

2 **Zoom** out to a full view of Earth with North facing up. Point out to students that Earth always appears in daylight in the **3D viewer**. To see a more realistic representation of Earth with shadows, click on the **sun tool** in the **Toolbar**. A **sun slider** will open in the upper left corner of the **3D viewer** and only part of Earth will be lit.

3 The default setting for the time span of the **sun tool** is one day. Move the **sun slider** left and right and ask students to follow the shadows on Earth over a day.

4 To change the time span, click on one of the **magnifying glass buttons** in the **sun slider**. Point out that each click of the **magnifying glass buttons** changes the time span displayed on the **sun slider** (one hour, one day, one week, one month, one year). Use the **magnifying glass buttons** to set the time span to one year.

* Tool introduced in this lesson

Shading the Earth *(cont.)*

Procedure *(cont.)*

5 Explain that Earth's axis is not straight up and down, but tilted at a 23° angle. Turn on the **Grid** under **View** in the **Menu Bar**. Use the **North-up button** to tilt Earth approximately 23°. Have students draw the line of axis, the Equator, the North and South Poles, and the Tropic lines on their activity sheets (question 1). Turn off the **Grid**.

6 Navigate to a view of Earth centered on the South Pole. Set the **sun slider** time span to one day. Click the **wrench icon** in the top-right corner of the **sun slider** to open the **Date and Time Options** and set the end date to December 21. Set the **Animation speed** to medium and click **OK**. Drag the **sun slider** all the way to the left and click the **play button** (it looks like a clock with an arrow) to watch the shadows move over the course of a day. Navigate to the North Pole and click the **play button** again.

7 Close the **sun slider**. Tell students that the tilt of Earth's axis is the reason we have seasons. Ask students to look at the second diagram on their activity sheets and answer questions 2 through 5.

8 Explorer Robert Peary reached the North Pole on April 7, 1909. **Fly to** and **placemark** Ellesmere Island, Nunavut, Canada, Peary's starting point. **Fly to** and **placemark** the North Pole and create a **path** of Peary's journey from Ellesmere to the North Pole. **Zoom** out to an **Eye alt** of about 16,000 km (10,000 mi.) and center the **path** in the **3D viewer.**

9 Click on the **sun tool** and set the time span to one day. Then, set the date to April 7. Click the **play button** and watch the shadows move over the course of the day. Have students answer questions 6 and 7 on their activity sheets.

10 **Fly to** and **placemark** the Royal Observatory, Greenwich, England. The Royal Observatory marks 0° longitude and is the world's reference clock. Time measure here is called Greenwich Mean Time (GMT).

11 Navigate to a global view (**Eye alt** about 8,850 km or 5,500 mi.) over the Greenwich **placemark**. Click the **wrench icon** in the **sun slider** to change the time zone to GMT in the **Specific time zone** drop-down menu. Keep the time span set to one day, the date as April 1, and move the **sun slider** to 1:00 A.M.. **Fly to** Hawaii. Have students answer question 8 on their activity sheets.

12 Ask students to write why they think it is important to have GMT (question 9).

Shading the Earth *(cont.)*

Extension Activity

Navigate to a view of Earth with the North Pole in the center of the **3D viewer**. Click the **sun tool**, reset the time period to one day, and set the date to December 21. Watch the shadows move over the course of a day and ask students to describe the conditions at the North Pole in December. Repeat these steps for the South Pole and for June 21.

Did You Know?

It appears in Google Earth that the Sun revolves around Earth, when in reality, Earth revolves around the sun in a year and rotates around its own axis in a day.

©2011 Google

Sun tool

©2011 Google

Sun slider

Screenshots

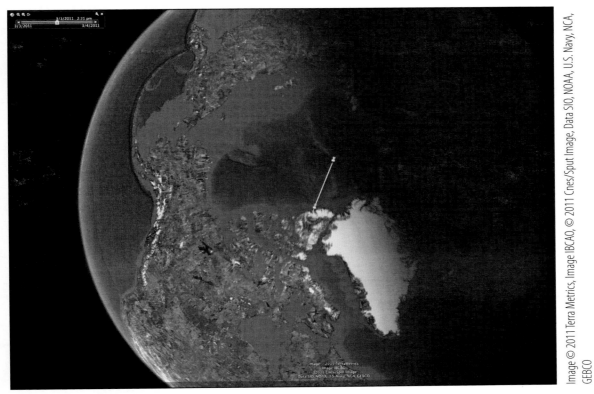

Image © 2011 Terra Metrics, Image IBCAO, © 2011 Cnes/Sput Image, Data SIO, NOAA, U.S. Navy, NCA, GEBCO

Peary's path to the North Pole

Name_____ Date _____

As the World Turns

- The Earth's axis is tilted 23°. Draw the line of axis in the diagram below.

- Draw and label the Equator as perpendicular to the line of axis.

- Label the North and South Poles.

- Draw a line of latitude at 23° North and label it Tropic of Cancer. Draw a line of latitude at 23°S South and label it Tropic of Capricorn.

As the World Turns *(cont.)*

2 Write what season it would be for each position of Earth relative to the sun (shown below) if you were standing on Earth at the location of the star.

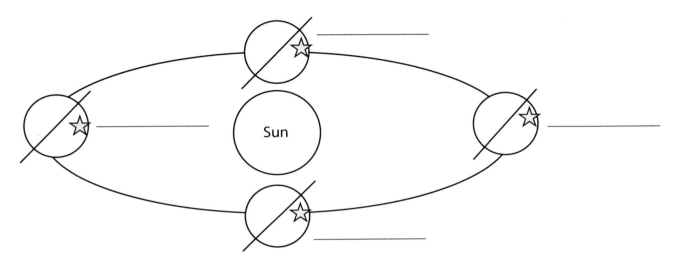

Sun

3 What season is it at the North Pole when it is winter at the South Pole?

_____

4 Do you think there are seasons at the Equator?

_____

_____

5 What is the significance of the Tropic lines?

_____

_____

_____

As the World Turns (cont.)

6 Create a path that indicates Peary's journey from Ellesmere Island to the North Pole. Watch the shadow over the course of April 7th. What were the light conditions during Peary's journey?

_____

_____

_____

_____

7 Why do you think Peary chose to travel to the North Pole in April?

_____

_____

_____

_____

8 Look at Greenwich, England, centered at 1:00 A.M. Fly to Hawaii. Is it day or night in Hawaii when it is the middle of the night in Greenwich?

_____

_____

_____

_____

9 Why do you think it is important to have Greenwich Mean Time (GMT)?

_____

_____

_____

_____

Using Energy

Google Earth Tools

- Toolbar: Clock, Placemark
- Layers panel: Borders and Labels, Roads
- Layers panel: Global Awareness: Appalachian Mountaintop Removal*

Overview

Students will understand that the sun is ultimately responsible for most of our energy sources and will explore these sources of energy in Google Earth, including renewable and nonrenewable.

Vocabulary

- compressed
- decompose
- diatoms
- fossil fuels
- nonrenewable
- renewable

Materials

- *Energy to Burn* activity sheets (pages 173–174)

Procedure

1 Tell students that the sun warms the planet, provides light, and helps plants grow. If we burn wood for heat, we are essentially getting that heat energy from the sun. If we eat vegetables, the energy that fuels our bodies is originally from the sun.

2 Distribute copies of the *Energy to Burn* activity sheets (pages 173–174) to students. On their activity sheets, have students list different sources of energy they use to help them run their lives and where they think each one comes from (question 1).

3 Explain that coal and oil come from swamp forests and tiny sea creatures, called diatoms, that existed before and during the time of the dinosaurs. The swamp forests and diatoms were buried, and over time they decomposed and were compressed in the earth until they became coal and oil. Now, they are being dug up and used to power homes, cars, and toys. That is why we classify coal and oil as fossil fuels. Ask students to write a definition of fossil fuels in their own words on their activity sheets (question 2).

* Tool introduced in this lesson

Using Energy (cont.)

Procedure (cont.)

4 Many coal mining operations are visible in Google Earth. In the **Layers panel**, turn on **Borders and Labels**, then open **Global Awareness** and turn on the **Appalachian Mountaintop Removal layer**. Double-click on the layer to navigate to the North Carolina/Virginia region. Point out the multiple icons that indicate the locations of the mountaintop mines and have students answer question 3 on their activity sheets.

5 Double-click on the overlay icon (two overlapping squares) labeled "Montgomery Creek, KY." An **Appalachian Mountaintop Removal window** will open with before and after pictures of the Montgomery Creek area. Click on **before** in the window to view Montgomery, Kentucky, before moutaintop removal.

6 Turn off the **Appalachian Mountaintop Removal layer** in the **Temporary Places folder** in the **Places panel** and **zoom** in to the Montgomery Creek mine. Use the **clock tool** to look back to 1995 and compare the area of excavation from the past to the present. On their activity sheets, ask students to write some possible impacts of mountaintop removal on the local environment (question 4). Close the **clock tool**.

7 **Fly to** and **placemark** the Antelope Coalmine, Douglas, Wyoming (43 28 15.78 N 105 20 21.27 W). Ask students to describe the area around the mine (question 5). **Fly to** and **placemark** the two other mines listed on the activity sheet and have students write descriptions of the mines. In question 6 on their activity sheets, have students write how these areas compare to the area surrounding the Montgomery Creek mine.

8 Explain to students that burning coal produces heat, water vapor, and carbon dioxide. The heat is used to make electricity. **Fly to** Drax, Britain, and **zoom** in on the coal-fired power plant (just to the northwest of town). Show students the white, billowing clouds of water vapor. Tell them that the colorless carbon dioxide goes into the atmosphere and becomes a greenhouse gas.

9 Tell students that coal and oil are nonrenewable sources of energy, which means that once they have been used, they are gone forever. There are renewable alternatives, such as geothermal energy that captures heat from under the surface of the Earth. **Fly to** Mammoth Lakes, California. Look about 3 miles east of town for the Mammoth Pacific geothermal plant (37 38 45 N 118 54 34 W).

Using Energy *(cont.)*

Procedure *(cont.)*

 10 Tell students that we can use the energy of the sun through solar panels that catch the sun's energy and convert it into electricity. **Fly to** Google Headquarters, Mountain View, California, to see solar panels on the roofs of buildings.

 11 **Fly to** Altamont Pass, California, turn on the **Roads layer,** and look to the north and south of Highway 580 for large wind turbines (wind farms) at an **Eye alt** of 300 m (1,000 ft.) or closer. Have students write the difference between renewable and nonrenewable sources of energy in their own words (question 7).

Extension Activity

Placemark these oil fields: Al Uthmaniya to Haradh, Saudi Arabia (24 49 14 N 49 14 11 E); Denver City, Texas (32 57 52 N 102 49 45 W); Prudhoe Bay, Alaska (70 14 12 N 148 30 07 W). Have students find common characteristics of oil fields.

Screenshots

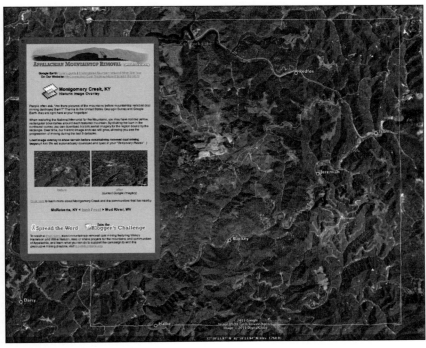

Appalachian Mountaintop Removal window

Using Energy *(cont.)*

Screenshots *(cont.)*

Antelope Coalmine, Wyoming

Image ©2011 DigitalGlobe, ©2011 Google

Name_____ Date _____

Energy to Burn

1 In the first column of the chart below, list different sources of energy that help you run your life. In the second column, write where you think these energy sources come from.

Source of Energy	Where It Comes From

2 Write a definition of *fossil fuels* in your own words.

_____

_____

3 Turn on the Appalachian Mountaintop Removal layer and look for the Appalachian Mountaintop Removal icons. Which states have mountaintop removal coal mines?

_____

4 Use the clock tool to look at the Montgomery Creek Mine in 1995. Move the timeline slider to the right to move forward in time. What are some possible impacts of mountaintop removal to the local environment?

_____

_____

_____

_____

Energy to Burn *(cont.)*

5 Describe the area surrounding the three mines listed below.

Mine Location	Description
Antelope Coalmine, Douglas, Wyoming 43 28 15.78 N 105 20 21.27 W Eye alt 4.5 km (15,000 ft.)	
Wuhai City, Inner Mongolia, China region 39 20 N 106 55 E Eye alt 12 km (40,000 ft.)	
Kusmunda, India 22 20 N 82 34 E Eye alt 1.3 km (4,500 ft.)	

6 Compare the areas in the chart above to the area surrounding the Montgomery Creek mine. How are they similar? How are they different?

_____

_____

_____

7 What is the difference between renewable and nonrenewable sources of energy?

_____

_____

_____

Measuring America

Standards
Students understand the characteristics and uses of spatial organization of Earth's surface. Students use proportional reasoning to solve mathematical and real world problems.

Google Earth Tools

- Status bar: Eye alt
- Toolbar: Polygon*
- Toolbar: Placemark. Ruler

Overview

Students will observe the results of The Ordinance of 1785 in North Dakota and use mathematical calculations to understand how the land was measured and organized.

Vocabulary

- aligned
- converged
- correction
- section
- survey

Materials

- *Plots of Land* activity sheets (pages 179–180)
- chart paper
- highlighters

Procedure

 1 Distribute copies of the *Plots of Land* activity sheets (pages 179–180) to students and open Google Earth.

 2 Tell students that the U.S. Land Ordinance of 1785 was adopted by Congress to raise money to pay for the Revolutionary War by selling the territory west of the original 13 colonies. Before the territory could be sold, the land had to be surveyed. With students, brainstorm a definition for survey, and have students add it to their activity sheets (question 1).

 3 To survey the land, parcels had to be measured and organized. A parcel is a defined piece of land. Have students look at the measurement and organization options on their activity sheets and write a pro and a con for each option (question 2).

 4 **Fly to** Fargo, North Dakota, and look at the farmlands to the west of Fargo at an **Eye alt** of about 24 km (15 mi.). This land was surveyed under The Ordinance of 1785. Based on observations of the farmlands, ask students to write how they think this land was measured and organized (question 3).

* Tool introduced in this lesson

Measuring America *(cont.)*

Procedure *(cont.)*

5 **Fly to** Buffalo, North Dakota (west of Fargo), and **zoom** to an **Eye alt** of about 8 km (25,000 ft.). Tell students that the Ordinance of 1785 said land would be surveyed into townships 6 miles long on each side, with each township divided into 36 sections. Point out the way the land is divided. Ask students to determine the length and width of one section (question 4). Use the **ruler tool** to measure the length and width of a section to verify its size.

6 Tell students there are 640 acres in a section. If a section is divided into quarters, it is called a quarter section, and if a quarter is again divided into quarters, it is called a quarter-quarter section. Have students determine how many acres are in a quarter-quarter section (question 5).

7 Click the **polygon tool** in the **Toolbar**. Use the **polygon tool** to draw a **polygon** around the section containing Buffalo, North Dakota. Center the cursor over the southwest corner of the section and click once, then, move the cursor to the southeast corner and click again. Repeat these steps for the northeast and northwest corners. A white square will appear in the **3D viewer**. In the **Polygon window**, click on the **Style, Color tab** and select 0% for opacity of the **Area**. Choose

a bright color for the **Lines** and increase the line width so you can clearly see your **polygon**. Then, click **OK** to close the **Polygon window**. Save the **polygon** to your *Geometry* folder.

8 Explain that within a township, sections were numbered starting with the section in the northeast (upper right) corner as number 1, then in ascending order moving west along the top row, east along the next row, and so on. Have students number the sections on their activity sheets and highlight the section containing Buffalo (question 6).

9 Based on the location of Buffalo, have students direct you to section 1 to draw a **polygon** around.

10 Click on the **ruler tool** in the **Toolbar**. Place the cursor on the southwest corner of the Buffalo section. Measure and move east 4.8 km (3 mi.), and then north 6.4 km (4 mi.). (You should be at **lat/long** 46 58 40.13 N 97 29 36.04 W.) Point out the jog, or irregularity, in the road and how the sections north and south of County Road 32 are not aligned. This is called a correction. It represents an adjustment in the surveying to account for the fact that lines of longitude converge as they head north.

Measuring America *(cont.)*

Procedure *(cont.)*

 11 **Placemark** this correction. Ask students to find two more corrections. Use the **ruler tool** to determine how far apart the corrections are in kilometers/ miles, in number of townships, and in number of sections (question 7).

Extension Activity

Fly to Falkland, North Carolina, at an **Eye alt** of about 9 km (30,000 ft.). Look at the patterns of the fields. This land was settled before the Revolutionary War. Show students how the fields are arranged in random patterns depending on how each farmer and his neighbors divided up the land.

Did You Know?

The point of origin for surveying the country was at the intersecting borders of Ohio, Pennsylvania, and West Virginia, north of the Ohio River, in the town of East Liverpool, Ohio. The first surveys were not perfect, as some of the land had already been settled. More and more of the land was completely surveyed into square sections and townships as they moved west.

Measuring America *(cont.)*

Screenshot

Buffalo, North Dakota

Name_____   Date _____

Plots of Land

1 Write a definition for *survey*.

_____

2 In early America, government officials had to decide how to measure and organize parcels of land. Look at the four options below and write one pro and one con for each option.

Measurement System	
Divide the land into parcels that could be divided by 10 Pro _____ _____ Con _____ _____	Divide the land into parcels that could be divided by 4 Pro _____ _____ Con _____ _____
Organization System	
Divide the land into organized squares, like a quilt Pro _____ _____ Con _____ _____	Divide the land to follow the geographical features, such as mountains and rivers Pro _____ _____ Con _____ _____

3 Fly to Fargo, North Dakota, and look at the farmlands to the west of Fargo at an Eye alt of about 24 km (15 mi.). This land was surveyed under The Ordinance of 1785. Based on observations of the farmlands, how do you think this land was measured and organized?

_____

_____

Plots of Land *(cont.)*

 4 The Ordinance of 1785 said land would be surveyed into townships 6 miles long on each side, and that each township would be divided into 36 sections. Use the chart below to determine the length of the sides of one section.

Township = 6 miles long on each side

Township = 36 sections

Each section is _____ mile(s) wide × _____ mile(s) long

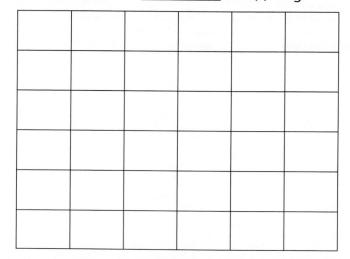

 5 Each section is 640 acres. If a section is divided into quarters, it is called a *quarter section*, and if a quarter is again divided into quarters, it is called a *quarter-quarter section*. How many acres are in a quarter-quarter section?

_____

 6 Within a township, sections were numbered starting with the section in the northeast (upper right) corner as number 1. Number the sections in the chart above by moving west along the top row, then east along the next row, and so on. Highlight the section containing Buffalo.

 7 Use the navigation tools to travel south from Buffalo and look for two corrections, starting at lat/long 46 58 40.13 N 97 29 36.04 W. Use the ruler tool to determine how far apart the corrections are in miles, in number of townships, and in number of sections. Write your answers in the chart below.

Correction location	Distance to Next Correction in Miles	Distance to Next Correction in Number of Sections	Distance to Next Correction in Number of Townships

Building a Capital

Standards
Students understand the symbolic importance of capital cities.
Students understand geometric transformation of figures.

Google Earth Tools

- Layers panel: Borders and Labels, Places
- Status bar: Eye alt
- Toolbar: Placemark, Polygon, Ruler

Overview

Students will use Google Earth to observe the layout of Washington, DC, calculate the sizes of various figures within the city, and create scale drawings of those figures.

Vocabulary

- rhombus

Materials

- *A Capital Idea* activity sheets (pages 184–186)

Procedure

1 Distribute copies of the *A Capital Idea* activity sheets (pages 184–186) to students and open Google Earth.

2 **Fly to** Washington, DC, **zoom** to an **Eye alt** of about 5 km (16,000 ft.), and navigate so that the National Mall is across the bottom of the **3D viewer** (see the screenshot on page 183). Ask students to describe some of the geometric shapes they see in the streets of the city.

3 Turn on the **Borders and Labels layer** and the **Places layer**. **Fly to** and **placemark** the White House, Scott Circle Park, and the Historical Society of Washington, DC. **Zoom** until all three **placemarks** are visible in the **3D viewer**. Use the **polygon tool** to make a triangle connecting these three points. Measure each side of the triangle in kilometers using the **ruler tool** and have students record the measurements on their activity sheets (question 1).

4 Use the **ruler tool** to determine the base and height of the triangle. Then, have students use the measurements to calculate the area of the triangle (question 2).

Building a Capital *(cont.)*

Procedure *(cont.)*

5 Tell students to use the side of the triangle connecting the White House and Scott Circle Park as an axis of symmetry and reflect the triangle along this axis. Have students determine which landmark will become the third point of the new triangle (question 3). **Zoom** in on this landmark and hover your cursor over the tree icon to find its name.

6 Draw the reflected triangle using the **polygon tool** in Google Earth. Ask students to use the information they have to estimate the area of the rhombus formed by joining the triangles (question 4). Save the polygon in a *Geometry* folder.

7 Have students identify the diagonals of the rhombus, using the chart on their activity sheets, and record the landmarks at the end of each diagonal (question 5). Measure the diagonals of the rhombus using the **ruler tool** and have students record the measurements to complete the chart. Then, ask students to calculate the area of the rhombus (question 6). Have students compare the calculated area of the rhombus to their estimate from question 4. Discuss their estimation techniques and accuracy.

8 Have students create a scale drawing of the rhombus on the grid on their activity sheets (question 7). The scale is one square = .25 kilometers.

9 Have students identify another shape formed by the streets of Washington, DC. Tell them to record the names of the landmarks at the corners of the shape and the measurements of the sides (question 8).

10 Have students write the name of the shape they discovered and calculate its area (question 9). Then, have students create a scale drawing of the new shape (question 10).

Extension Activity

Ask students which two important buildings are connected by Pennsylvania Avenue and the two branches of government these buildings house. Search for the building that houses the third branch of government and ask students, based on the original layout of Washington, DC, whether the Supreme Court was considered to be as important as the President and Congress.

Building a Capital *(cont.)*

User Tip

If using an interactive whiteboard, have students use the pen tool to trace some of the shapes and patterns formed by the city streets.

Did You Know? ✕

Pierre Charles L'Enfant was commissioned by George Washington to design Washington, DC. He was a fan of mathematics and used his math skills to make a very creative city with avenues radiating out from rectangles.

Screenshot

Washington, DC

Name_____ Date _____

A Capital Idea

 1 Use the ruler tool to measure the distances between the Washington, DC landmarks listed below. Record the measurement for each distance in kilometers.

Landmarks	Distance Measurement
The White House to Scott Circle Park	
Scott Circle Park to The Historical Society of Washington, DC	
The Historical Society of Washington, DC to The White House	

2 Calculate the area of the triangle formed by connecting these landmarks.

Formula: area $= \frac{1}{2}bh$ (where b is base, and h is height)

$b =$ _____

$h =$ _____

Area = _____

 3 When this triangle is reflected along the line of symmetry (White House to Scott Circle), what landmark becomes the third point of the new triangle?

_____

 4 Estimate the area of the rhombus created by joining the two triangles.

Area = _____

A Capital Idea *(cont.)*

5 In the chart below, write the names of the landmarks that are each end of the diagonals of the rhombus. Record the lengths of the diagonals in kilometers.

Landmarks at Each End of Diagonal	Length of Diagonal

6 Calculate the area of the rhombus.

Formula: $\dfrac{d_1 d_2}{2}$ (where *d* is diagonal)

Area = _____

Was your estimate correct? _____

7 Make a scale drawing of the rhombus on the grid below.   ☐ .25 km

A Capital Idea *(cont.)*

8 Find a 3- or 4-sided shape formed by the streets of Washington, DC. Record the landmarks at the corners of this shape. Record the measurements of each side in kilometers.

Landmarks at Each End of Diagonal	Length of Side

9 Calculate the area of the shape.

Area = _____

10 Make a scale drawing of the shape you found. ☐ .25 km

Adding Up Algebra

Standards

Students know how human activities have increased the ability of the physical environment to support human life in the local community, state, United States, and other countries.

Students understand and apply basic and advanced properties of functions and algebra.

Google Earth Tools

- Status bar: elev
- Toolbar: Ruler

Overview

Students will continue to explore Google Earth and use mathematics to understand the role of a park ranger.

Vocabulary

- circumference
- radius

Materials

- *Park Ranger Notebook* activity sheets (pages 190–192)

Procedure

1. Tell students they can use Google Earth to imagine what it is like to be a park ranger. Open Google Earth and **Fly to** Egmont National Park, New Zealand. Look for the park's centerpiece, a volcano called Mt. Taranaki. Show students how the vegetation on Mt. Taranaki changes abruptly from agricultural to forest at the base, which is also the edge of the park. Discuss with students why they think the edge of the park is delineated so sharply.

2. Distribute copies of the *Park Ranger Notebook* activity sheets (pages 190–192) to students and open Google Earth. Tell students the first thing they need to do as a park ranger is to measure the volcano. Tell students to use in meters and kilometers for all their measurements because the country of New Zealand uses the metric system as their system of measurement.

3. Click on the **ruler tool** in the **Toolbar**. In the **Ruler window**, set the units to kilometers. Click on a spot at the outside edge of the park, then move the cursor toward the center of the volcano until the distance reads approximately 2 km. Have students read the **elev** in the **Status bar** and record it on their activity sheets (question 1).

Adding Up Algebra *(cont.)*

Procedure *(cont.)*

4 Measure 4 km, 6 km, and 8 km from the outside edge of the park toward the center of the volcano and have students record each **elev** in the chart on their activity sheets. The summit of the volcano is approximately 10 km from the southwest edge. Have students determine snf record the elevation at 10 km as well.

5 Have students create coordinates using the table of measurements on their activity sheets. The distance from the outside edge is the *x*-coordinate and the corresponding elevation is the *y*-coordinate for each point (question 2).

6 Have students plot the points on the coordinate grid (question 3) and draw the graph of the line (question 4).

7 Tell students that as park rangers, they might be asked about the slope of the volcano by hikers interested in climbing it. Using the formula on the activity sheet, have students use the highest and lowest elevation points to calculate the slope (question 5).

8 Tell students they will need to know the circumference of the park and how long it will take to walk around its circumference to check the park boundary. Use the **ruler tool** to find the approximate radius of the park (question 6). Have students use the formulas on their activity sheets to estimate the circumference (question 7). (**Note:** Use the circular area of the park. Do not include the small cinder cone to the northwest of the park.)

9 Tell students to calculate how long it would take to walk this distance, assuming an average speed of 5 km per hour (question 8).

Extension Activity

Use the techniques for mapping a volcanic park to map Capulin Mountain in the Capulin Volcano National Monument in New Mexico. Open the **More layer** in the **Layers panel** and turn on the **Parks/Recreation Areas layer** to see the outline of the park and estimate the percent of the park's area that is covered by the volcano.

Adding Up Algebra *(cont.)*

User Tip

Students will be using metric measurements in this lesson so you will need to set the **elev** display in the **Status bar** to metric units. Click **Google Earth** in the **Menu Bar**, select **Preferences**, and under the **3D View tab**, set **Show Elevation** to **Meters, Kilometers**. In the **Ruler window**, use the pull-down menu to select meters.

Did You Know?

Mt. Tarankai is one of the most symmetrical volcanoes in the world. The cone on the northwest face is called Fantham's Peak after a nineteen-year-old girl who climbed to the summit in 1887 while wearing full Victorian dress.

Screenshot

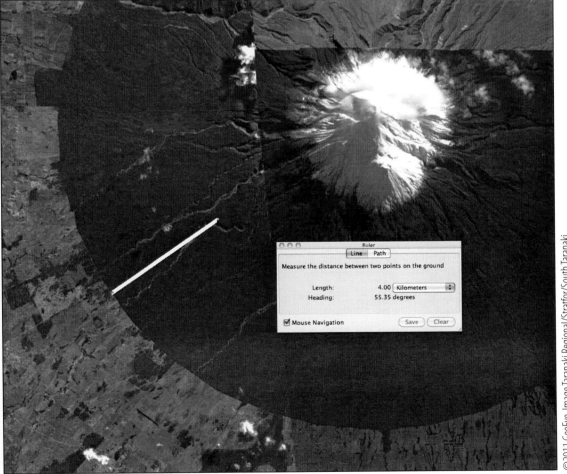

©2011 GeoEye, Image Taranaki Regional/Stratfor/South Taranaki

Measuring Mt. Taranaki, New Zealand

Name_____ Date _____

Park Ranger Notebook

Directions: Imagine you are a park ranger at Egmont National Park in New Zealand. It is your responsibility to know as much as possible about Mt. Taranaki, the volcano at the center of the park. Answer the following questions.

1 Use the ruler tool to measure from the outside edge of the park toward the center to each of the following distances. Distances do not need to be exact. Record the elevation at each approximate distance.

Distance from Outside Edge (in km) x-coordinate	Elevation (in m) y-coordinate
2 km	
4 km	
6 km	
8 km	
10 km (summit)	

2 Use each set of measurements to create coordinates. For example, a distance of 2 km and an elevation of 530 m would be the point (2, 530) on the grid.

(_____ , _____)

(_____ , _____)

(_____ , _____)

(_____ , _____)

(_____ , _____)

3 Plot each point on the grid on the next page.

4 Draw a line through the coordinates on the grid.

Park Ranger Notebook *(cont.)*

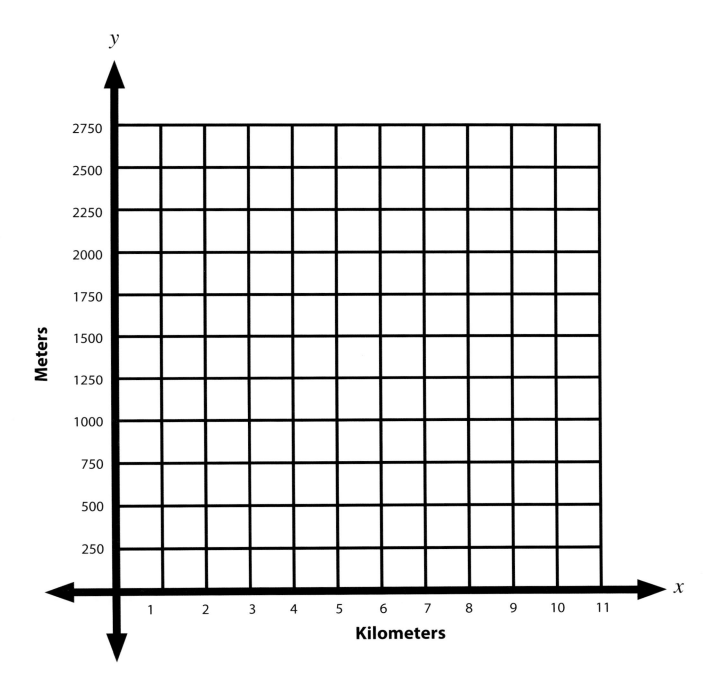

Park Ranger Notebook *(cont.)*

 5 Use the highest and lowest elevation points in the formula below to find the slope of the line.

(m = slope)

$$m = \frac{(y_2 - y_1)}{(x_2 - x_1)}$$

$m =$ _____

 6 Use the ruler tool to measure the approximate radius of Egmont National Park.

(r = radius)

$r =$ _____ km

 7 Use the following formulas to determine the circumference of Egmont National Park.

Diameter = $2r$

Diameter of Edgemont Park = _____ km

Circumference = πd (d = diameter, $\pi \approx 3.14$)

Circumference of Edgemont Park = _____ km

 8 Estimate how long it would take to walk the circumference of Egmont National Park, assuming an average speed of 5 km per hour.

_____

Subtracting the Amazon

Standards
Students know the causes and effects of changes in a place over time.
Students select and use appropriate estimation techniques.

Google Earth Tools
- Layers panel: Global Awareness: UNEP: Atlas of Our Changing Environment*
- Status bar: Eye alt
- Toolbar: Polygon

Overview
Students will use Google Earth to estimate deforestation in the Amazon.

Vocabulary
- deforestation

Materials
- *Deforestation* activity sheets (pages 197–198)

Procedure

1. Distribute copies of the *Deforestation* activity sheets (pages 197–198) to students and ask them to read the first passage. Ask students to write in their own words what they think this passage means (question 1).

2. Open Google Earth and **Fly to** Powhatan, Virginia, at an **Eye alt** of 8 km (25,000 ft.). This area was deforested during Benjamin Franklin's lifetime. Ask students to compare the colors of the forested and deforested areas. Then, ask students to answer question 2 on their activity sheets.

3. Tell students that an area of global concern today is the deforestation of the Amazon Basin. Open the **Global Awareness layer** in the **Layers panel** and turn on the **UNEP: Atlas of Our Changing Environment layer**. **Fly to** Brazil. As you **zoom** in, you will see **UNEP icons** in the northwest region of Brazil. Look for the **UNEP icon** labeled "Rondonia" and **zoom** in on it until the square of forest outlined in orange fills the **3D viewer**.

* Tool introduced in this lesson

Subtracting the Amazon *(cont.)*

Procedure *(cont.)*

4 Click on the **UNEP icon** and choose the **Overlay Images in Google Earth** option. You will see two new image overlays in the **Temporary Places folder** from September 2001 and June 1975. Turn on both layers and click once on the **19 June 1975 layer** in the **Places panel** to highlight it. Move the **Places slider** (just beneath the **Places panel**) to fade back and forth between the two layers. Ask students to write their observations on their activity sheets (question 3). Turn off both overlay images.

5 **Zoom** in on the west side of the orange **UNEP rectangle** to a darker rectangle (**lat/long** 10 3 7 S 64 8 13 W) at an **Eye alt** of about 40 km (25 mi.). The darker color indicates that a high-resolution image is available. Tell students that this section of forest will be their sample area for the remainder of this activity.

6 Use the **polygon tool** to outline this area of forest. Under the **Style, Color tab** in the **Polygon window**, choose a color for the lines that will outline the **polygon**. Under the **Area** section, select **Outlined** from the pull-down menu. Name the **polygon** *Sample* and save it.

7 **Zoom** to a view in which the *Sample* **polygon** fills the **3D viewer**. Turn on the **19 June 1975 layer** in the **Temporary Places folder** and ask students to note that in 1975, no forest had been cleared.

8 Turn off the 1975 layer. Then, turn on the **19 September 2001 layer** and ask students to estimate the percent of forest that has been cleared within the sample area outlined by the **polygon** and record the percentage on their activity sheets (question 4).

9 Tell students they will use the percentage of forest cleared in their sample to estimate the number of acres cleared in the Amazon forest in 2001. Tell students that the total area of the Amazon forest is 5.5 million km². Have students multiply the total area of the forest (5,500,000 km²) by the percent of forest cleared in the sample they observed. This will give them an estimate of the amount of land cleared in the entire Amazon forest (question 4).

Subtracting the Amazon *(cont.)*

Procedure *(cont.)*

 10 Ask students how many years elapsed between the taking of the 1975 image and the 2001 image. Have students divide the estimated amount of cleared Amazon forest by the number of years between images to estimate the number of km² cleared per year. Have them write their answers on their activity sheets (question 4).

 11 Tell students that Brazil's National Institute for Space Research (NISR) estimates that in 2004, deforestation rates were at their peak at more than 27,000 km² per year. By 2009, deforestation had fallen to around 7,000 km² per year. Have students enter their yearly estimate of land cleared on the chart on their activity sheets (question 5). Ask them to look at the chart and then make a prediction of how much Amazon forest will be cleared in 2014. Tell them to write a paragraph explaining their prediction (question 6).

User Tip

Remind students that they are only making estimates using a very small area. Scientists can actually measure deforestation using satellite images that cover the entire Amazon Basin and computer programs that automatically recognize change in the forest due to clearing.

Extension Activities

- Ask students to estimate the percent of deforestation per year for the following regions: Madagascar (15 45 S 47 16 E) Oregon (43 45 N 123 21 W) Bolivia (16 52 S 63 53 W)

- Have students research the effects of deforestation on our environment. If deforestation continues at the present rate, what are some possible consequences for Earth?

Did You Know? ⊗

Explain that, like burning coal, burning wood converts long-term carbon storage to atmospheric carbon dioxide (CO_2). If forests are cut and replanted, they remain a carbon storage. If new forests are planted, the amount of carbon dioxide in the atmosphere is reduced.

Subtracting the Amazon *(cont.)*

Screenshot

Rondonia UNEP overlay and sample area near Rondonia, Brazil

Name_____ Date _____

Deforestation

Directions: Read the passage below. Then answer the following questions.

"By clearing America of woods," Benjamin Franklin wrote, Americans were "Scouring our Planet— and so making this Side of our Globe reflect a brighter Light to the Eyes of the Inhabitants of Mars or Venus" (quoted in Williams, M.). However, it was not the inhabitants of Mars or Venus that were likely to be affected by the newly bright land, the prescient weatherman noted, it was the very Americans who were carving farms out of the forest. Franklin and other colonists agreed in 1763 that "cleared land absorbs heat and melts snow quicker," but Franklin believed that years of observations would be necessary before anyone could make any conclusion about the effect of deforestation on local climate. He was right. In 2008, 245 years later, scientists are just beginning to understand how much land use can change the weather.

(Steyaert and Knox 2008)

1 In your own words, write what you think this passage means.

_____

_____

_____

2 Compare the colors of the forested and deforested areas in Powatan, Virginia. Which area most likely absorbs more energy from the sun, the cleared land or the forested land? Why do you think so? (*Hint:* Think about which is more comfortable on a hot day: a light-colored shirt or a dark-colored shirt?)

_____

_____

_____

3 Write what you observe about the deforestation of Rondonia between 1975 and 2001.

_____

_____

_____

Deforestation *(cont.)*

4 Follow the steps below to calculate an estimate of the rate of deforestation in the Amazon.

- Estimate the percent of forest cleared in the sample between 1975 and 2001.
- *Approximately _____ % of the sample has been cleared.*
- The total area of the Amazon forest is approximately 5,500,000 km². Use the data from your sample (above) to estimate the total amount of forest cleared in the Amazon between 1975 and 2001.
- *Approximately _____% of the sample cleared x 5,500,000 km² = _____ km² of Amazon forest cleared*
- Divide your answer by the number of years between images to estimate the amount of Amazon forest cleared each year.
- *_____ km² of Amazon forest cleared ÷ _____ years = _____ km² cleared each year*

5 Enter your estimate in the first row (2001) of the chart below. Using the information in the chart to help you, make a prediction about how much Amazon forest will be cleared in the year 2014.

Amazon Deforestation	
Date	**Estimated Amount Cleared per Year**
2001	
2004	27,000 km² per year (NISR estimate)
2009	7,000 km² per year (NISR estimate)
2014	

6 Write a paragraph explaining your prediction.

_____

_____

_____

_____

_____

_____

_____

_____

_____

_____

Exploring Mars

Standards
Students know that astronomical objects in space are massive in size and are separated from one another by vast distances.

Google Earth Tools
- Fly to box: lat/long
- Layers panel: Featured Satellite Images*
- Layers panel: Global Maps: Colorized Terrain*
- Layers panel: Mars Gallery: Rovers and Landers*
- Status bar: Eye alt
- Toolbar: Planets: Mars*

Overview
Students will travel from the Earth to Mars to explore the landing sites for the rovers Spirit and Opportunity as well as the craters, volcanoes, and canyons on Mars.

Vocabulary
- fly by
- lander
- orbiter
- rover
- sample return

Materials
- *To Mars* activity sheets (pages 203–204)

Procedure

1. Tell students that with Google Earth, it is possible to explore more than just Earth. They can also explore the Moon, Mars, and the celestial sky.

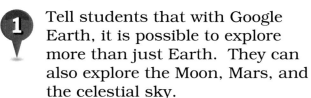

2. Distribute copies of the *To Mars* activity sheets (pages 203–204) to students. Ask students to work with partners to research and define the vocabulary words listed in question 1. Ask students what all these terms have in common.

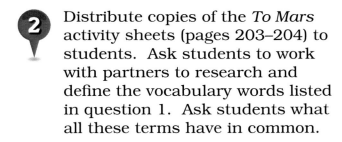

3. Ask students if they think there is life on Mars and how they could tell. Have them write their ideas on their activity sheets (question 2)

4. Open Google Earth and turn off all **placemarks**, folders, and layers in the **Places panel** and **Layers panel**. Click on the **planets tool** in the **Toolbar** and select **Mars**.

5. **Zoom** in to an **Eye alt** of about 1,600 km (1,000 mi.) and use the **Move joystick** to look around the planet. Ask students to note any interesting features they observe on their activity sheets (question 3).

* Tool introduced in this lesson

Exploring Mars *(cont.)*

Procedure *(cont.)*

6 **Fly to** 23 20 38 S 87 06 49 E at an **Eye alt** of 115 km (70 mi.). Explain to students that they can tell that one crater is younger than another because an older crater is overlapped by a younger crater.

7 **Fly to** Olympus Mons. Tell students that Olympus Mons is a large volcano. Use the **zoom slider** and the **Look joystick** to get different perspectives of the volcano. **Placemark** Olympus Mons and save it to a *Mars* folder.

8 **Zoom** out to an **Eye alt** of 800 km (500 mi.) and use the **ruler tool** to measure the diameter of Olympus Mons, using the ring as its base. Then, have students determine the height of Olympus Mons using the **elev** display and record the diameter and elevation of Olympus Mons on their activity sheets (question 4). Return to Earth using the **planets tool**. **Fly to** Mount Ranier, Washington, and measure its diameter, using the snow boundary as its base, and elevation (question 5). Have students compare the differences in diameter and elevation of Olympus Mons and Mount Ranier (question 6).

9 Return to Mars using the **planets tool**. Turn on the **Featured Satellite Images layer** in the **Layers panel** and look for the **Featured Satellite Images icons** (red and yellow squares). **Zoom** in and click on the icons to explore and learn about these regions that were photographed from orbit at a very high resolution.

10 Tell students that two rovers, Opportunity and Spirit, landed on Mars in 2004. These rovers were designed to last one year, but Opportunity worked until at least 2011 and Spirit worked until 2009. Open the **Mars Gallery layer** in the **Layers panel**. Then, open the **Rovers and Landers layer** and turn on the **MER Opportunity Rover layer**. **Fly to** Victoria Crater.

11 **Zoom** close to Cape Verde and Duck Bay on the edge of Victoria Crater and click on the **camera icon** labeled "'Panorama from 'Cape Verde.'" Tell students that this photo was taken by the Opportunity Rover.

12 In the **Panorama window**, click on **Fly into this high-resolution photo**. Controls similar to the **navigation tools** for viewing the panorama are in the upper right corner of the **3D viewer**. (***Note:*** You may need to hover your cursor over the top third of the **3D viewer** to make the controls appear.) Have students describe the features listed on their activity sheets (question 7).

Exploring Mars *(cont.)*

Procedure *(cont.)*

13 Click **Exit Photo** and **zoom** out so that Mars fills the **3D viewer**. Open the **Global Maps layer** and turn on the **Colorized Terrain layer**. Mars will become colorful.

14 Point out the **Color Scale** in the lower left corner. Explain to students that the colors represent elevations, resulting in the creation of a colorful topographic map of Mars that emphasizes its terrain. Ask students which colors represent the highest and lowest elevations (question 8). Ask students to use color to identify Olympus Mons.

Extension Activity

Spirit landed on Mars on January 4, 2004, and became stuck on May 1, 2009. Although Spirit still operates, it can no longer rove. If Spirit could be freed, where should it go on its next mission? Find Spirit. Use the **path tool** to draw a **path**, and use **placemarks** to select three new stops. Write a description of its stops and goals.

Did You Know?

Evidence of running water has been discovered on Mars. The NASA webpage (http://www.nasa.com) contains an article titled "NASA Images Suggest Water Still Flows in Brief Spurts on Mars," as well as many other interesting facts about this planet.

Screenshots

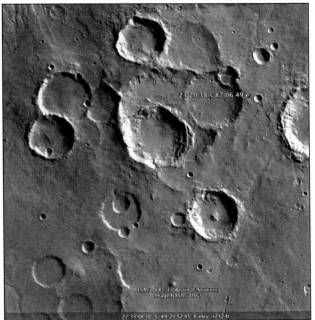

Image NASA/USGS, ESA/DLR/FU Berlin (G.Neukum)

Mars craters

Exploring Mars *(cont.)*

Screenshots *(cont.)*

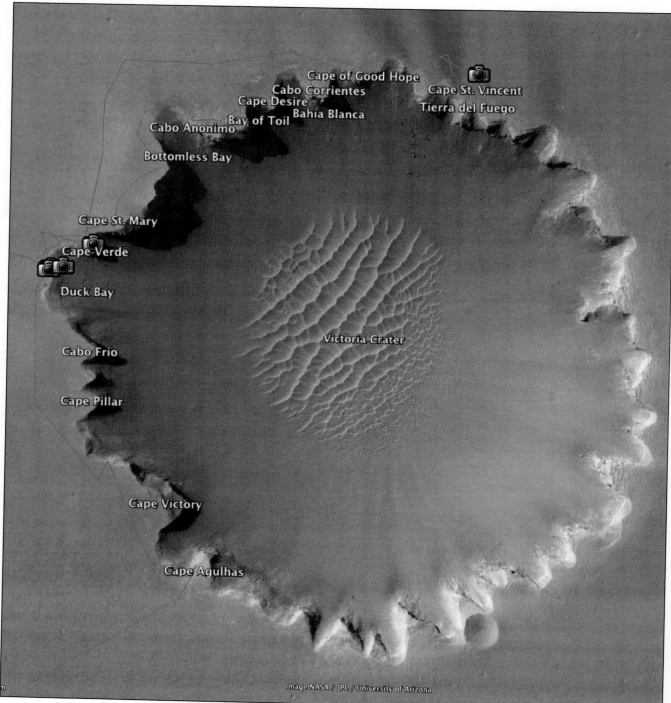

Victoria Crater

Name_____ **Date** _____

To Mars

1 Work with a partner to research and define the following terms:

- fly by _____

- lander _____

- orbiter _____

- rover _____

- sample return _____

2 Do you think there is life on Mars? How could you tell? What evidence would you look for?

_____

_____

_____

_____

_____

3 In Google Earth, look at Mars at an Eye alt of about 1,600 km (1,000 mi.) and use the Move joystick to look around the planet. Write down any interesting features you observe.

_____

_____

_____

_____

To Mars *(cont.)*

4   Use the ruler tool to measure the diameter and elevation of Olympus Mons on Mars.

diameter: _____

height: _____

5   Use the ruler tool to measure the diameter and elevation of Mount Rainier in Washington.

diameter: _____

height: _____

6   What are the differences in diameter and elevation between Olympus Mons and Mount Rainier?

difference in diameter: _____

difference in height: _____

7   Fly to the Opportunity Rover. Look at the panorama view called "Panorama from 'Cape Verde.'" On the lines below, describe what you see.

_____

_____

_____

8   Look at the Colorized Terrain map of Mars.

Which color represents the highest elevation?_____

Which color represents the lowest elevation? _____

Migrating with Whales

Standard
Students know ways in which organisms interact and depend on one another through food chains and food webs in an ecosystem.

Google Earth Tools
- Earth Gallery: Chlorophyll*
- Earth Gallery: Sea Surface Temperature*

Overview
Students use false color maps of ocean properties to explore why gray whales migrate and how the whales are part of a complex food chain.

Vocabulary
- amphipods
- false color
- food chain
- migrate
- phytoplankton

Materials
- *Why Whales Migrate* activity sheets (pages 209–210)
- markers or colored pencils

Procedure

 1 Ask students to share with the class what they know about whales. Tell students that in this lesson, they will learn about the migration of gray whales off the west coast of the United States. Distribute copies of the *Why Whales Migrate* activity sheets (pages 209–210) to students and open Google Earth.

 2 Tell students that gray whale calves begin their lives in lagoons in Baja, California. **Fly to** the three lagoons (listed below) where gray whales give birth, and explore each lagoon using the **navigation tools**. **Placemark** each lagoon.

- Laguna Ojo de Liebre, Baja California, Mexico (27 51 43.66 N 114 14 3.67 W)

- Laguna San Ignacio, Baja California, Mexico (26 49 23.99 N 113 12 42.99 W)

- Laguna Magdalena, Baja California, Mexico (24 35 57.49 N 111 56 2.34 W)

 3 Tell students that even whales have primary predators like killer whales. Ask students to write why they think whales choose to have their calves in lagoons instead of the open ocean (question 1).

* Tool introduced in this lesson

Migrating with Whales *(cont.)*

Procedures *(cont.)*

 4 The whales stay in the lagoons from about January through March and then begin their migration north. Mark the whales' migration by **placemarking** one of the Baja lagoons as the starting point and the Bering Sea as the final destination. Name these **placemarks** according to the migration months they represent (*January–March* for the Baja lagoon, *August–October* for the Bering Sea.) Additionally, **placemark** four other points along the migration path using the locations listed below. Name each **placemark** according to the migration month that it represents and save the placemarks to a *Whale Migration* folder.

- April—ocean off San Diego, California
- May—ocean off Point Piedras Blanca, California
- June—ocean off Oregon
- July—ocean off Kodiak Island, Alaska

 5 Use the **path tool** in the **Toolbar** to connect the **placemarks** and show the whales' migratory path. Check the **Measurements tab** in the **Path window** to see how far the whales migrate.

 6 Tell students that gray whales head north during the northern hemisphere summers to feed on crustaceans called amphipods. Amphipods are abundant in the shallow waters of the Bering Sea because phytoplankton is abundant. The amphipods feed on the phytoplankton, and the gray whales feed on the amphipods, and sometimes killer whales feed on gray whales. Ask students to draw this food chain on their activity sheets (question 2).

 7 Satellites can map the whales' food sources by measuring chlorophyll, which is in phytoplankton. These measurements are presented as chlorophyll concentration in a false color map. To view the false color map of chlorophyll levels, search for "chlorophyll" in the **Earth Gallery**. Under "World and Regional Ocean Chlorophyll" click on **Open in Google Earth**. Turn on and double-click the **World and Regional Chlorophyll layer** in the **Temporary places panel**. (***Note***: This layer may take some time to load.) **Zoom** out until you see the entire Earth. Green areas indicate more chlorophyll and phytoplankton, and blue and pink areas indicate less chlorophyll and plankton.

Migrating with Whales *(cont.)*

Procedures *(cont.)*

8 Compare the chlorophyll levels in the Bering Sea with those in the ocean off Baja California to see why the gray whales head north. Have students color the map on their activity sheets to show the chlorophyll levels. Have students draw an arrow pointing north along the migratory route on the map and label it "food" (question 3).

9 Another false color map shows students why the whales head south again for the winter. Turn off the **Chlorophyll layer**. Open the Earth Gallery and search for "sea surface temperature." Under "World and Regional Sea Surface Temperatures" click on **Open in Google Earth.** Turn on and double-click the **World and Regional Sea Surface Temperatures layer** in the **Temporary places panel**. (**Note**: This layer may take some time to load.) This is a false color map of the surface temperature of the ocean. Red is warmer and blue is colder.

10 Ask students why they think the whales migrate south to give birth to their calves. Have students draw an arrow pointing south along the migratory route on the map and label it "temperature" (question 4).

Extension Activity

You can follow the migration path of a fin whale by opening the **Animal Tracking layer** in the **Ocean layer** and looking for the whale off Lompoc, California. Click on the whale to read more about fin whales and click on **Download track** to follow this whale.

Screenshots

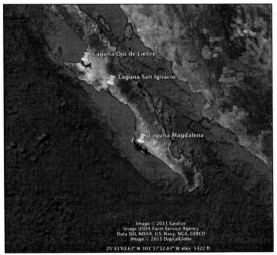

Lagoons in Baja

Migrating with Whales *(cont.)*

Screenshots *(cont.)*

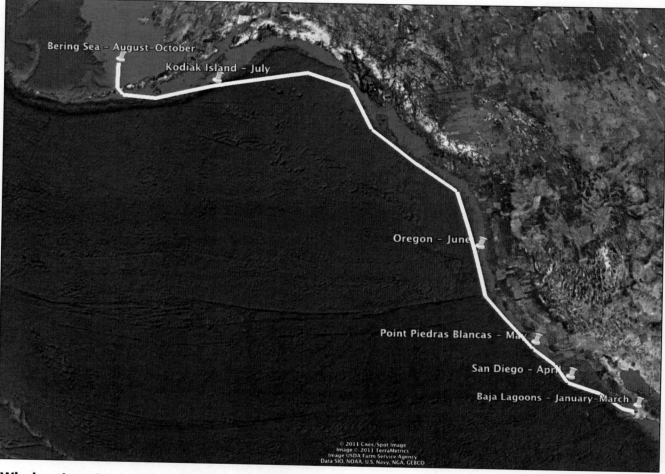

Whale migration path from Baja, California to the Bering Sea

Name _____ Date _____

Why Whales Migrate

1 Why do you think whales choose to have their calves in lagoons instead of the open ocean?

_____

_____

2 Draw a representation of the food chain including gray whales, amphipods, phytoplankton, and killer whales.

Why Whales Migrate *(cont.)*

 Color the map below to show chlorophyll levels as displayed in the Google Earth false color map. Draw an arrow showing the direction that gray whales migrate in the summer for food. Label the arrow "food."

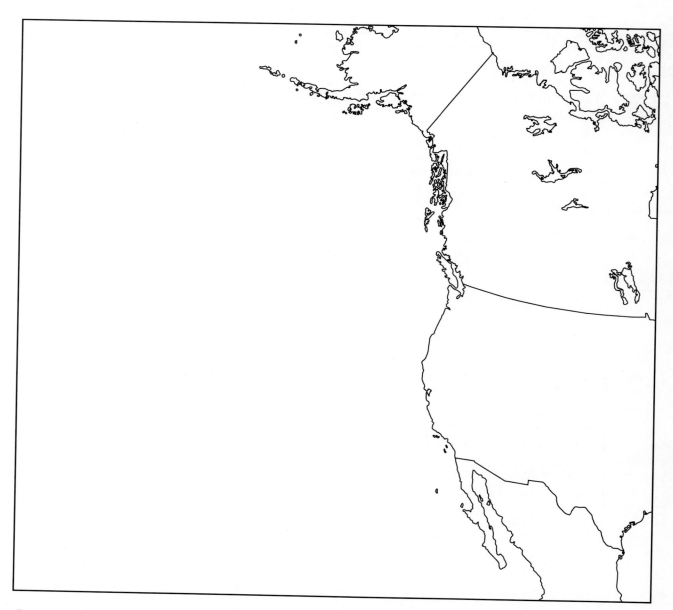

 Draw another arrow on the map showing the direction gray whales travel in the winter toward warmer temperatures. Label the arrow "temperature."

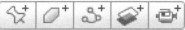

Observing Population

Standards

Students understand distributions of physical and human occurrences with respect to spatial patterns, arrangements, and associations.

Google Earth Tools

- Layers panel: Borders and Labels
- Layers panel: Gallery: NASA: Earth City Lights*

Overview

Students will investigate the population distribution of the world using Google Earth to display lights on Earth at night.

Vocabulary

- composite
- dense
- megalopolis
- sparse

Materials

- *People Here and There* activity sheets (pages 214–216)

Procedure

 Ask students if they live in a big city with a dense population, or a rural area with a sparse population. Discuss why some areas have greater populations than others. Distribute copies of the *People Here and There* activity sheets (pages 214–216) to students. Tell students that a megalopolis is a very large urban city. In their own words, have students define megalopolis (question 1).

 Open Google Earth. In the **Layers panel**, open the **Gallery layer**, open the **NASA layer**, and turn on the **Earth City Lights layer**. Ask students what they observe in the **3D viewer**. Tell students that despite what they see, Earth could not really be dark all at one time. Explain that this view of Earth is a composite of images taken at night and collected over a long period of time.

 Tell students that lights on Earth can be used as indicators of large populations and economic development. Have students discuss why, in some cases, a dense population might not appear as a bright area at night. Have them respond on their activity sheets (question 2).

* Tool introduced in this lesson

Observing Population *(cont.)*

Procedure *(cont.)*

4 **Fly to** Egypt at an **Eye alt** of about 1,200 km (800 mi.) and look at the distribution of lights. Ask students what the lights reveal about the population distribution of Egypt (question 3).

5 **Fly to** to the United States at an **Eye alt** of about 3,500 km (2,000 mi.) and ask students to compare the coastal regions to the inland regions. Then, have them compare the eastern and western coastlines of America (questions 4 and 5). Ask students to identify a megalopolis.

6 Turn on the **Borders and Labels layer** in the **Layers panel**. **Fly to** each of the seven continents and look for megapolises by zooming in on locations with bright lights until the name of the city appears. On their activity sheets, have students list three major megapolises from each continent using this method (question 6).

7 Divide the class into groups and ask the groups to investigate and compare night lights in the following areas:

- eastern and western China
- North Korea and South Korea
- coastal Africa and inland Africa

Extension Activity

Ask students to research and compare the populations of two countries, or two regions within one country, using the **Earth City Lights layer** in Google Earth. Have students write an essay comparing the factors that contribute to population growth or decline in each country or region.

Did You Know? ✕

The images in the **Earth at Night layer** were taken by the Defense Meteorological Satellite Program's (DMSP) Operational Linescan System (OLS). This network of satellites was originally designed to pick up on lunar illumination reflecting off of clouds at night in order to aid nighttime aircraft navigation. What the Air Force discovered is that on evenings when there was a new moon, the satellites were sensitive enough to record the illumination from city lights. Over a period of several new moons, the data the satellites retrieved could be pieced together to produce a global image of city lights.

Observing Population *(cont.)*

Screenshot

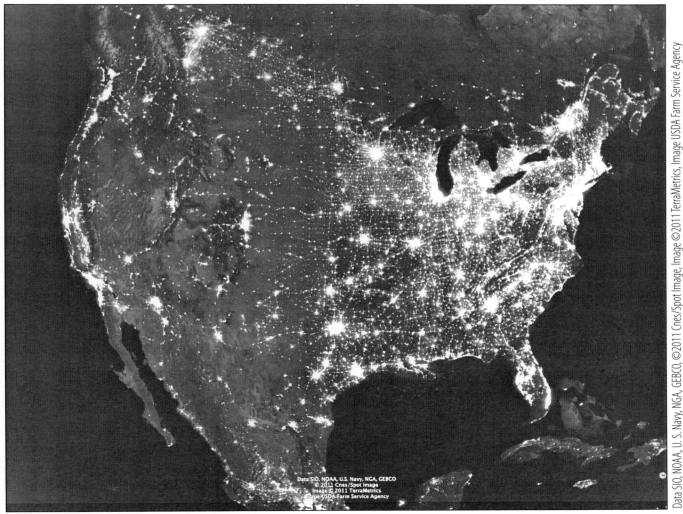

United States city lights

Name_____ Date _____

People Here and There

1 Define *megalopolis*.

_____

_____

_____

2 Look at the view of a Earth using the Earth City Lights layer. Are lights the only indicators of populated areas? Why or why not?

_____

_____

_____

3 Fly to Egypt and look at the distribution of lights. What do the lights reveal about the population distribution of Egypt?

_____

_____

_____

_____

_____

People Here and There *(cont.)*

4 Fly to the United States at an Eye alt of about 3,540 km (2,000 mi.) with the Earth City Lights layer turned on. Then, answer the following questions.

Compare the coastal regions to the inland regions. What do you notice?

_____

_____

_____

_____

_____

5 Compare the eastern and western coastlines of America. What do you notice?

_____

_____

_____

_____

_____

People Here and There *(cont.)*

6 Turn on the Borders and Labels layer. Fly to each of the seven continents and zoom in on regions with bright lights until the names of the cities appear. For each continent, list the names of three megapolises and their countries.

North America

_____

_____

_____

South America

_____

_____

_____

Europe

_____

_____

_____

Australia

_____

_____

_____

Asia

_____

_____

_____

Africa

_____

_____

_____

Antarctica *(none)*

Discovering Places

Standards
Students understand the ways in which technology influences the human capacity to modify the physical environment.

Google Earth Tools
- Fly to box: lat/long
- Status bar: Eye alt
- Toolbar: Ruler

Overview
Students will investigate archaeological discoveries using Google Earth.

Vocabulary
- fish trap
- geoglyph
- impact crater

Materials
- *Overhead Discoveries* activity sheets (pages 220–222)

Procedure

1. Ask students to name some well-known archaeological discoveries. Point out that most (if not all) of these discoveries were made by someone who traveled to the site of the discovery. Today, scientists can use images taken from the air or space to look for undiscovered archaeological and natural features, including ancient cities along the Silk Road, ancient rivers in Egypt, impact craters, Mayan settlements in Mexico, and even Noah's Ark.

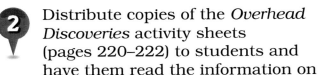

2. Distribute copies of the *Overhead Discoveries* activity sheets (pages 220–222) to students and have them read the information on aerial archaeology.

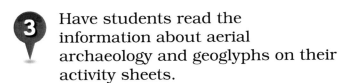

3. Have students read the information about aerial archaeology and geoglyphs on their activity sheets.

4. **Fly to** 8 50 38.40 S 67 15 11.73 W, a geoglyph in Brazil, at an **Eye alt** of about 2 km (6,600 ft.). Have students read the information about the geoglpyh, then measure and record the size and archaeological indicators of the geoglyphs in the chart on their activity sheet (question 1). Have them write a brief description of the geoglyph as well.

Discovering Places *(cont.)*

Procedure *(cont.)*

5 Fly to the other geoglyphs listed below and have students read the descriptions, record the measurements and indicators, and describe the geoglyphs (questions 2 and 3).
- Saudi Arabia: 22 17 51.05 N 40 27 42.18 E, **Eye alt** 2 km (6,600 ft.)
- England: 51 21 22.17 N 1 50 03.44 W, **Eye alt** 1 km (3,200 ft.)

6 Ask students what other kinds of lines can be seen on Earth from above, and have them list these on their activity sheet (question 4). Discuss what criteria archaeologists might use to distinguish geoglyphs and other archeological artifacts from other types of lines and shapes. Have students write about what they think distinguishes geoglyphs from other lines they may see on Earth.

7 **Fly to** 52 06 32.78 N 4 42 27.83 W and **zoom** to an **Eye alt** of 700 m (2,300 ft.) over the v-shaped artifact in the bay. Tell students that this artifact was first spotted in photographs taken from an airplane and then identified by archaeologists with the help of Google Earth in 2007. Ask students what they think this archeological artifact might be.

8 Have students read the description of the fish trap in question 5 on their activity sheets. **Zoom** in and use the **ruler tool** to measure the size of this artifact. Ask students if it is larger or smaller than they thought it might be. How does is compare to the size of their school? Have them record the size of the fish trap on their activity sheets and write a description of the artifact (question 5).

9 **Fly to** 16 16 49.57 S 36 21 47.35 E and **zoom** to an **Eye alt** of 25 km (15 mi.). Have students read the paragraph about Mt. Mabu in question 6 on their activity sheets. Measure the bright green forested area and have students record this information on their activity sheets. Have students write a paragraph explaining why it is important to protect areas like Mt. Mabu (question 6).

Did You Know? ⊗

Many photographers have added their collection of photographs to the **Layers panels**. J. Michael Fay collected aerial photographs of villages and African animals from a little red airplane. These photos can be found in the **Gallery layer** under the **National Geographic Magazine layer**, under the **African Megaflyover layer**.

Discovering Places (cont.)

Screenshot

Ancient fish trap, Wales

Name_____ Date _____

Overhead Discoveries

Directions: Read the information below and use it to help you answer the questions on the following pages.

Aerial archaeology is the process of observing archaeological features from the air. Archaeologists can get different information looking at a find from above than they can on the ground. When looking at an archaeological feature from above, there are four different types of indicators to look for.

- **Shadow marks** can reveal raised archaeological features. Viewing shadow marks requires the sun to be at an angle, rather than straight overhead.
- **Cropmarks** are differences in the color, height, or texture of crops due to differences in the ground beneath them.
- **Frostmarks** are visible in winter where water pools and freezes in the lines of buried features.
- **Soilmarks** are the differences in soil color between the natural terrain and archaeological features.

Geoglyphs are large man-made shapes or designs on Earth. Often they cannot be distinguished from ground level. Many were discovered by aerial photography in which archaelologists could see indicators such as shadow marks, cropmarks, frostmarks, and soilmarks.

Satellite imagery, like that used in Google Earth, has made it possible to identify geoglyphs more easily over a larger area than with aerial photography. Geoglyphs can be found in many areas of the world.

 In South America, clearcutting of the rainforest has exposed geoglyphs that were obscured by vegetation. So far, scientists using Google Earth have identified more than 200 geoglyphs stretching over 250 km in the Amazonian basin. They are thought to be between 1,000 and 2,500 years old, and many think that these geoglyphs are indications of an as-yet unknown ancient South American civilization.

Fly to and look at the geoglyph at the location listed in the chart and fill in the information.

Location	Size	Indicators	Description
Brazil 8 50 38.40 S 67 15 11.73 W Eye alt 2 km (6,600 ft.)			

Overhead Discoveries *(cont.)*

 A professor in Australia has identified almost 2,000 geoglyphs in Saudi Arabia using Google Earth, without ever leaving his office. Most of these sites are in remote or inaccessible areas and have not been observed by scientists in person.

Fly to and look at the geoglyph at the location listed in the chart and fill in the information.

Location	Size	Indicators	Description
Saudi Arabia 22 17 51.05 N 40 27 42.18 E Eye alt 2 km (6,600 ft.)			

 In England, thousands of Stone, Bronze, and Iron Age sites such as barrows, burial mounds, cairns, and henges are visible in Google Earth. New sites are being found all the time.

Fly to and look at the geoglyph at the location listed in the chart and fill in the information.

Location	Size	Indicators	Description
England 51 21 22.17 N 1 50 03.44 W Eye alt 1 km (3,200 ft.)			

4 List some other kinds of lines you see on Earth in Google Earth, besides geoglyphs.

_____

_____

Describe how an archaeologist might distinguish between geoglyphs and other kinds of lines when searching for research sites in Google Earth.

_____

_____

_____

_____

_____

_____

Overhead Discoveries *(cont.)*

This stone fish trap is now completely under water, but when it was built the stone walls were submerged at high tide and exposed at low tide. As the tide went out, fish became stranded in the trap and were then scooped out with nets. This fish trap is very large and is estimated to be over 1,000 years old. It probably took a great number of people to construct it. Today, the walls of the trap are below the surface of the water even at low tide, so fish can no longer be trapped.

Fly to and look at the location listed in the chart and fill in the information.

Location	Size	Description
Wales 52 06 32.78 N 4 42 27.83 W Eye alt 700 m (2,300 ft.)		

In 2005, a team of scientists used Google Earth to identify the area of Mount Mabu in Mozambique, Africa, as a potential conservation site because of its isolation and seemingly untouched forest. In 2008, a team hiked in to the forest to identify species and collect samples. They found many rare and exotic plants and species, including three unknown species of butterfly and a new species of poisonous snake. They are now working with the government of Mozambique to protect the area.

Fly to and look at the location listed in the chart and fill in the information.

Location	Size	Description
Mozambique 16 17 56 S 36 23 40 E Eye alt 7 km (20,000 ft.)		

Why do you think it is important to protect places like Mt. Mabu?

_____

_____

_____

_____

References Cited

Bean, T. 2010. *Multimodal learning for the 21st century adolescent.* Huntington Beach, CA: Shell Education.

Card, S. K., J. D. Mackinlay, and B. Shneiderman. 1999. *Readings in information visualization: Using vision to think.* San Francisco, CA: Morgan Stanley Kaufmann Publishers.

Castiglione, C. 2009. New media project: Information visualization. Unpublished report.

Common Core State Standards for English Language Arts. 2010. http://www.corestandards. org/the-standards/ Accessed August 25, 2011.

Conklin, W. 2007. *Applying Differentiation Strategies.* Huntington Beach, CA: Shell Education.

———. 2011. *Activities for a Differentiated Classroom.* Huntington Beach, CA: Shell Education.

Frei, S., A. Gammill, and S. Irons. 2007. *Integrating technology into the curriculum.* Huntington Beach, CA: Shell Education.

Image Science and Analysis Laboratory, NASA-Johnson Space Center. "The Gateway to Astronaut Photography of Earth." http://eol.jsc.nasa.gov. Accessed August 22, 2011.

Maggio, Alice. 2003. Measuring a Chicago mile. Gapers Block: Ask the Librarian. http://www.gapersblock. com/airbags/archives/measuring_a_ chicago_mile/. (Oct. 2.)

NASA Earth Observatory. The Earth Observatory Science Project Office. http://earthobservatory. nasa.gov/GlobalMaps/. Accessed August 22, 2011.

Roschelle, J., R. Pea, C. Headley, D. Gordin, and B. Means. 2001. Changing what and how children learn in school with computer-based technologies. *The Future of Children* 10(2): 76–101.

Science Education Resource Center (SERC). 2009. Why teach with Google Earth™? Starting Point: Teaching Entry Level Geoscience. http://serc. carlton.edu. Accessed July 20, 2011.

Shultz, R. B., J. Kerski, and T. Patterson. 2008. The use of virtual globes as a spatial teaching tool with suggestions for metadata standards. National Council for Geographic Education. *Journal of Geography* 107: 27–34.

Silverstein, G., J. Frechtling, and A. Miyaoka. 2000. *Evaluation of the use of technology in Illinois public schools: Final report.* Rockville, MB: Westat.

Taylor, Frank. 2005. Google Earth Files—KML/KMZ. *Google Earth Blog.* September 15. http:// www.gearthblog.com/blog/ archives/2005/09/google_earth_ fi.html. Accessed Aug. 25, 2011.

Answer Key

Learning to Fly

Looking Down (pages 34–36)

1. Student's descriptive adjectives will vary.

2. Students should have colored their maps to match the colors of the globe in Google Earth. Students should have labeled one desert, island, forest, and ocean.

3. green: *forest or vegetation*

   blue: *water, oceans*

   brown: *mountains, cleared land*

   tan: *desert*

   white: *snow or ice*

4. Students' descriptions will vary, but may describe how the horizon looks flat while viewing Earth from ground level, and the view from the whole globe appears curved.

Schools Around the World (pages 41–42)

1. Students' answers will vary, but may include:

   Rural: Fields, farms, trees, not many house

   Urban: Lots of buildings, cars, trucks, public transportation

   Suburban: Tract homes, recreational areas

2. Students' responses will vary, but should indicte which type of community they live in and list some of its characteristics.

3. Students should have written the address of their school.

4. Students' responses will vary, but should describe three features of their school.

5. Students should have written the name of each school and a description in each circle of the Venn diagram. In the overlapping sections, they should list any features that the two schools have in common. In the middle section, they should list features all three schools have in common, such as buildings and sports fields.

6. Students' paragraphs will vary.

The Gift of the Nile (pages 46–48)

1. Students' responses will vary, but should describe the Nile River and how its waters flow north to the Mediterranean Sea.

2. delta—a sediment-filled landform at the mouth of a river where river water flows over the land

   floodplain—flat land adjacent to a river that stretches from the banks of the river to the base of the enclosing valley walls, and experiences flooding during high water

3.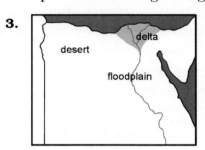

4. canals or pipes

5. The pyramids and tombs would be safe from floods but still close to the Nile.

Cultural Symbols (pages 52–54)

1. Students' responses will vary, but features of the bridge may include a toll booth, lanes for traffic, suspension cables passing through the main towers, orange in color, and pedestrian accessible.

2. Students' responses will vary, but features of the Opera House may include the white vaulted shell-like roof steps, a terrace for pedestrians, and two main halls side by side.

3. The Pritzker Prize

4. Students' responses will vary, depending on whether they feel the architect was deserving of the Pritzker Prize.

5. The Washington Monument is tall obelisk with a pyramid-shaped roof and a circular terrace surrounding it.

6. Icons appear for metro stations, museums, monuments, parks, and federal buildings.

7. Responses may vary.

8. Belvedere Rd., Westminster Bridge Rd., Bridge St., St. Margaret St.

Answer Key *(cont.)*

Seeing Earth

Artificial Evidence (pages 58–60)

1. Natural features: river, lake volcano

   Artificial features: crop, canal, town, bridge, road, building, reservoir, trail

2. Students' responses may vary.

3. About 10 km or 36,000 ft.

4. Eye alt of typical passenger plane: yes

   Eye alt of International Space Station: no

   Eye alt of Apollo on the Moon: no

5.

Structure	Last Eye alt when the feature was still visible	Visible from Space Station?
Arecibo Observatory, Arecibo, Puerto Rico	~210 km (140 mi.)	No
John F. Kennedy Space Center, Florida	~450 km (280 mi.)	Yes
Palm Islands, Dubai, United Arab Emirates	~900 km (560 mi.)	Yes
Panama Canal, Panama	~370 km (230 mi.)	Yes
Hoover Dam, Nevada	~35 km (21 mi.)	No
Suez Canal, Egypt	~400 km (250 mi.)	Yes
Palmanova Udine, Italy	~140 km (90 mi.).	No
Indianapolis Motor Speedway, Indiana	~40 km (25 mi.)	No

6. Highway BR163 provided road access to the Amazon forest, allowing developers to come in and cut the forest for agriculture.

An Elevated View (pages 64–66)

1. volcano   lake

   river   grassland

   forest   glacier

2. Elevation: the height of land surface above sea level

3. Highest elevation: ~5,800 m (19,000 ft.) Actual peak elevation is 5,895 m (19,341 ft.)

   Lowest elevation: ~1,200 m (4,000 ft.)

4. Height: ~4,500 m (15,000 ft.)

5. Vegetation can only grow on land surfaces up to a certain elevation because the climate changes dramatically at higher elevations. Such factors as atmosphere, temperature, oxygen, sunlight, wind, moisture, and weather can all affect vegetation growth, making it difficult for plants to grow in higher regions.

6.

Location	Highest Elevation	Lowest Elevation	Describe the Feature
Grand Canyon, Arizona	~2.7 km (9,000 ft.)	~640 m (2,100 ft.)	Desert, dry land, canyons, river, some plants
Dead Sea, Israel/ Jordan	~30 m (100 ft.)	~ -415 m (-1,363 ft.)	Desert, dry land, ocean, no plants
Mt. Everest, Nepal	~8.8 km (28,800 ft.)	~4,300 m (14,000 ft.)	Ice, snow, bare rock, little to no vegetation
Redwood National Park, CA	~520 m (1,700 ft.)	~26 m (90 ft.)	Forest, dense vegetation

Answer Key *(cont.)*

Latitude and Longitude Lines (pages 70–72)

1.

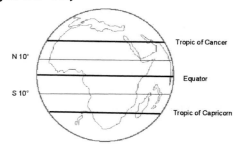

2. The middle latitude range should be green because it most likely gets the most amount of rain (N10° to S10°) while N10° to N30° and S10° to S30° should be tan because it most likely get the least amount of rain.

3. In Africa, there is more rain near the Equator.

4. The Hawaiian islands

5. The island of Hawaii

6. Mauna Kea Observatory

In Scale (pages 79–80)

1. Students' drawings will vary.

    Your school measurement - varies, depending on your school

    The Great Pyramid of Giza (diagonally)–310 m (1000 ft.)

    Spiral Jetty (diameter)–60 m (200 ft.)

2. through **5.**

    Comparisons to school in the third and fourth columns will vary.

Landmarks	Measurements
Your school	varies depending on your school
The Great Pyramid of Aiza, Egypt	310 m (1000 ft.)
Spiral Jetty, Utah	60 m (200 ft.)
The Coloseum, Rome	180 m (590 ft.)
Cadillac Ranch, Texas	60 m (195 ft.)
Victoria Falls, Zimbabwe	1700 m (5500 ft.)
Stonehenge, England	30 m (100 ft.)
Angkor Wat, Cambodia	1500 m (4,800 ft..)

Building My World

Sorting My World (pages 82–84)

1. Student's responses will vary.

2. Students' responses will vary.

3. Students' responses will vary.

Travel Time! (pages 88–90)

1. Students' responses will vary.

2. Students' responses will vary.

3. Students' itineraries will vary, but students should have listed the beginning and ending locations of their trip, and include three stops, bodies of water traveled, and modes of transportation needed to complete the trip.

4. Students' responses will vary.

5. Students' responses will vary.

Islands of War (pages 94–96)

1. Students' responses will vary, but should describe the landscape of the Navajo Nation, e.g., desert, some forestry, valleys, dry land, canyons, and river.

2. Students' responses will vary, but should describe the landscape of Guadalcanal, e.g., tiny island, narrow beaches, jungle, crops, rivers.

3. Students' responses will vary, but should describe Papua New Guinea's landscape, e.g., island, cloud-covered mountains, tropical rainforests, rivers, and narrow beaches.

4. Students' responses will vary, but should describe how Guadalcanal was a good location because of the narrow beaches and tropical forests.

5. Ned's home in Arizona is very different from the islands in the Pacific. Ned grew up in the inland desert, surrounded by dry land, canyons, valleys, and some forestry. The islands in the Pacific are very tropical and surrounded by the ocean, with rainforests, and beaches.

6. The islands in the Pacific were important in the U.S.'s war against Japan not only because the U.S. needed to have a connection to Australia, but also because

Answer Key *(cont.)*

the islands would have given the Japanese an advantage in launching attacks against the U.S. since the islands lie between Japan and the U.S. in the Pacific Ocean.

Circles (pages 101–102)

1. Radius = 600 m

   Diameter= 1,200 m

   Circumference = 3,800 m

   Area = 1,100,00 m^2

2. Measurements are approximate

Location	Diameter	Radius	Area
Manicouagan Crater	60 km	30 km	2,83 km^2
Meteor Crater	1.15 km	.58 km	1.04 km^2
Roter Kamm Crater	2.35 km	1.18 km	4.34 km^2
Wolf Creek Crater	.9 km	.45 km	.64 km^2

3. The average area of the impact craters is approximately 708.25 km^2

4. Measurements may vary but the diameters should be approximately 830 m and the circumferences approx. 2,607 m.

5. The average circumference should be approximately 2,607 m.

6. The average circumference of these circular fields indicates the average area that the irrigation's pivot system can effectively provide to water the fields' crops.

Language Arts

On the River (pages 109–110)

1. southeast or down river

2. Students' responses will vary, but should describe the geographical features of Fourmile Island, e.g., the river, rural farm land, vegetation, a shallow island, woods, no sign of articificial features.

3. So they could have more time and distance to cross the current to toward the island as the current carried them downstream.

4. Because he couldn't wade or swim to Missouri because of the current.

5. Students should have placemarked the location on their maps where the boys reached the Missouri shore. The boys could have hidden in the shrubbery, the woods, or tall plant life on the Missouri shore.

6. The setting of the Mississippi River is important to the story because it allowed the characters to quickly escape from danger, and escape is a major theme in the story.

Walk Two Moons (pages 112–114)

1. Students' responses may vary but could include: Quincy, Kentucky is a small town near the Ohio River, farms, grassy hills, and woodsy areas. Euclid, Ohio is a city and is near Lake Erie, suburban areas, and freeways. Both Quincy, KY and Euclid, OH are near significant bodies of water.

2. Euclid, OH, because it has fewer trees.

3. Location: Lake Michigan. Gram mistakenly thought they were near the ocean because they were actually near Lake Michigan, which is a large body of water similar to the size of a state.

4. Students' responses will vary.

5. The path from Euclid, OH to Lewiston, ID is approximately 1,900 miles.

Living History (pages 120–122)

1. Students' answers will vary, but may include the fact that Denmark is next to Germany and is accessible by both land and water.

2. Amalienborg Palace, Copenhagen: A large, open plaza surrounded by four large buildings; gardens near the river.

   Gilleleje, Denmark: A small city surrounded by farm fields on the edge of the sea across from Sweden.

3. Students' sequence maps will vary, but should include places that are significant to the story.

Answer Key *(cont.)*

My Preview (pages 124–126)

1. Students should list the title of a book read during a previous lesson, and the placemarks they chose for their tours which represent locations from the book's setting.

2. Students should have chosen three key locations that are significant to the story, and should have described these locations in detail.

3. Students' scripts will vary, but should serve as the narration of their tour.

4. Students' movie preview posters will vary. Check their posters' images and text for understanding.

Making Memories (pages 130–132)

1. Students should describe the appearance of Port-au-Prince prior to the earthquake.

2. Students should describe the appearance of Port-au-Prince after earthquake. Students should compare similarities and differences in the appearance of this area before and after the earthquake.

3. Students should cite the blue tent cities that sprung up around the Presidential Palace. These tents developed to serve as temporary housing for those who lost their homes in the quake.

4. No response required.

5. Students' responses will vary.

Pizarro's Journey (pages 136–138)

1. Surrounded by terrain or several sides of land to protect from harsh weather; deep water for large boats

2. Access to water, good climate for crops, moderate temperature.

3.

Location	Harbor	Settlement	Resources
Isthmus of Panama (Eye alt 322 km or 200 mi.)	X	X	X
Tumaco, Columbia	X		
Tumbes, Peru		X	X
Paita, Peru	X		X
Cajamarca, Peru (use lat/long 07 09 52 S 78 30 38 W)		X	X
Jauja, Peru		X	X
Cuzco, Peru		X	
Lima, Peru		X	

4. Tumbes and Juaja both have settlements and resources.

5. The geography of Jauja was not effective for trade because it was located high in the mountains and away from the ocean. Pizarro later relocated the capital of Peru to Lima because it was located near the coast.

6. An ancient abandoned city, known as Machu Picchu, sits atop the mountain. The structures appear to be almost built into the mountain. Steep valleys surround Machu Picchu and a switchback trail leads from the valley to the site. Abundant greenery and semi tropical vegetation grows around Machu Picchu.

7. 74 km (or 46 mi.)

8. Machu Picchu was difficult to find because it sits at a very high elevation on a mountain ridge 50 miles away from Cuzco. The hidden Incan city was probably not noticeable from ground level in the Urubamba Valley.

9. Students' tours and planning sheets will vary based on their three chosen locations.

Answer Key *(cont.)*

Roman News (pages 142–144)

1. Students' responses will vary but should list ancient Roman structures that still exist today.

2. Students' responses will vary but shoud list ancient Roman structures that no longer exist.

3. Students' responses will vary. Check students' work to verify each location and description match the appropriate newspaper sections.

4. Students' planning outlines will vary.

The Olympic Games (pages 148–150)

1. Students' timelines should include these places:
   - 2012–London, England
   - 2008–Beijing, China
   - 2004–Athens, Greece
   - 1984–Los Angeles, USA, boycott
   - 1980–Moscow, Russia, boycott
   - 1948–London, England
   - 1944–cancelled
   - 1940–cancelled
   - 1936–Berlin, Germany
   - 1916–cancelled
   - 1908–London, England
   - 1896–Athens, Greece

2. Students' answers may vary but should compare the three Greek stadiums.

3. Students should describe changes at all three stadiums listed in the chart.

4. During 1916, World War I was taking place. During 1940 and 1944, World War II was taking place. Students' responses will vary, but will most likely explain why the Olympics should have been cancelled during these time periods.

5. Cold War

5. Europe: 16
   Asia: 3
   Africa: 0
   Australia: 2
   North America: 6
   South America: 0
   Students' responses will vary.

Science

Glaciers and Sea Ice (pages 155–156)

1. Alaska–source in mountains, reaches sea, ridges parallel to flow, meets other glaciers

   Argentina–rough surface, ridges parallel and perpendicular to flow direction, reaches sea

   Fox–arc shaped ridges, flows into river, flows down valley

2. Students' responses may vary, but common characteristics among glaciers may include two of any of the following: located in polar regions, originate on land, occur at high elevations, begin at the top of high mountains and descend down, take up large amounts of space, surrounded by snow, etc.

3. Students' responses will vary, but could describe how the edges of ice sheets cover the all continental land, appear like steep mountain ranges, descend into the ocean, or are breaking off into the ocean water.

4. Icebergs: broken off pieces of glaciers or ice sheets; float in the ocean; formed from the bottom portion of glaciers that have reached the edge of a continent.

   Moraine: arched mounds of dirt that glaciers have pushed up against over several years, and have left behind after the glacier retreats; consists only of dirt and debris; exists on land; located around the surrounding areas of a glacier.

5. Students should have colored in yellow the extent of the Arctic Sea Ice in 1979 on their maps.

6. Students should have colored in red the extent of the Arctic Sea Ice in 2008 on their maps.

7. The sea ice has experienced around 40% loss since 1979.

8. Most of the glaciers from the past have significantly melted. The land is now covered with glacial lakes. More mountain ranges are exposed. Less snow and ice are present.

Answer Key *(cont.)*

Volcanoes (pages 160–162)

1. Students' responses will vary.
2. Convergent
3. Divergent
4. Transform
5. Students paragraphs will vary, but should detail the relationships between the plate tectonics, volcanoes, earthquakes, and landforms on Earth.

As the World Turns (pages 166–168)

1.

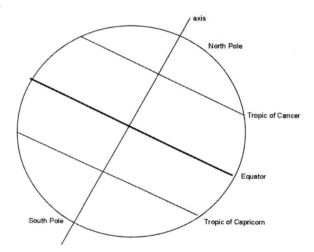

2.

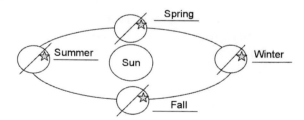

3. summer
4. No, the sun is always overhead.
5. Between the Tropic of Cancer and the Tropic of Capricorn, the sun shines directly overhead at least some of the year.
6. Peary would have been in the light all day and night.
7. Because the sun would be up for the entire summer ahead.

8. When it is 1:00 A.M. in Greenwich it is daytime in Hawaii.
9. It is important to have Greenwich Mean Time (GMT) because it is considered the world's reference time zone.

Energy to Burn (pages 173–174)

1. Students' responses will vary but may include:

   Sources of energy: coal, gas, oil, electricity

   Where it comes from: coal mines, underground, water, fossils, forests, oceans, volcanoes

2. Fossil fuels–natural fuel, such as coal or gas, formed in the geological past from the remains of living organisms.
3. West Virginia, Virginia, Kentucky, and Tennessee have mountaintop removal mines.
4. Because of mountaintop removal, there is noticeably less land, less vegetation, contaminated water sources, contaminated air, and therefore the environment cannot support as much local animal life.
5. Students' descriptions will vary, but may include:

Mine Location	Description
Antelope Coalmine, Douglas, Wyoming	The land looks really raw and exposed. There is no vegetation, and everything looks dead surrounding the area.
Wuhai City, Inner Mongolia, China	The area is very barren and dark. The land looks dried out with no life.
Kusmunda, India	This area has more bluish water and also darker coal exposed.

6. All the areas look devastated from the land excavation. The Montgomery Creek mountaintop removal site does not seem to have as much exposed elements as the three mine locations.

Answer Key *(cont.)*

7. Nonrenewable sources cannot be reproduced once used up. Renewable sources are reproducible and are less damaging to the environment.

Mathematics

Plots of Land (pages 179–180)

1. Survey–to determine the exact position and boundaries of an area of land using angular measurements and calculations.

2. Students' pros and cons will vary for each measurement system but could include:

Parcels divided by 10: pro–easy math; con–hard to quarter
Parcels divided by 4: pro–easy to quarter; con–hard math
Organized squares: pro–easy to sell; con–hard to survey on terrain
Organized by geography: pro–more river access; con–hard to survey

3. Organized squares/quilted pattern parcels divisible by 4.

4. Each section is one mile wide by one mile long.

5. There are 40 acres in a quarter-quarter section.

6.

6	5	4	3	2	1
7	8	9	10	11	12
18	17	16	15	14	13
19	20	21	22	23	24
30	29	28	27	26	25
31	32	33	34	35	36

7. Corrections at:

46 58 40.13 N 97 29 36.04 W

46 37 47 N 97 29 36 W

46 16 57 N 97 29 23 W

The corrections are 24 miles, 4 townships, or 24 sections apart from one another,

A Capital Idea (pages 184–186)

1.

Landmark	Distance Measurement
White House to Scott Circle	1.06 km
Scott Circle to the Historical Society of Washington, DC	1.3 km
The Historical Society of Washington, DC to White House	1.3 km

2. $b = 1.06$ km

$h = 1.15$ km

Area = .6095 km^2

3. Washington Circle Park

4. Area = 2 x .6095 km^2 = 1.22 km^2

5.

Landmarks at Each End of Diagonal	Length of Diagonal
Scott Circle Park to the Historical Society of Washington, DC	1.06 km
The Historical Society of Washington, DC to Washington Circle Park	2.3 km

6. Area = 1.22 km^2

7.

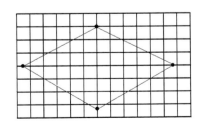

8. Students' responses will vary.

9. Students' responses will vary.

10. Students' responses will vary.

Answer Key *(cont.)*

Park Ranger Notebook (pages 190–192)

1. Measurements are rounded

Distance from Outside Edge (in km) x-coordinate	Elevation (in m) y-coordinate
2 km	500 m
4 km	700 m
6 km	1,000 m
8 km	1,600 m
10 km	2,400 m

2. (2, 500), (4, 700), (6, 1000), (8, 1600), (10, 2400).

3. and 4.

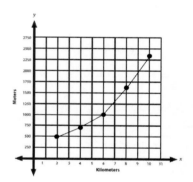

5. m = 237.5

6. Radius = 10 km

7. Diameter of Edgemont Park = 20 km
   Circumference of Edgemont Park = 60 km

8. 12 hours

Deforestation (pages 197–198)

1. Students' responses will vary.

2. The deforested land absorbs less energy because it does not have trees to help it absorb the sunlight and the lighter color of the land reflects sunlight.

3. In 1975, the entire area in Rondonia was covered with healthy forest. In 2001, the area had been heavily devastated by the effects of deforestation.

4. Students' estimates will vary. The NISR estimate is around 5,384,615.4 acres^2 per year.

5. Students should make a prediction about how much Amazon forest will be cleared in 2014 based on the results for 2001–2009.

6. Students responses will vary depending on students' deforestation estimates.

Beyond Earth

To Mars (pages 203–204)

1. fly by: the flight of a spacecraft when it comes close enough to a celestial body to gather data

   lander: a space probe designed to land on solid celestial bodies

   orbiter: a space probe designed to orbit around a celestial body

   rover: a small remote-controlled vehicle which roams over rough terrain, designed for taking photographs and gathering rock and soil samples from extraterrestrial bodies.

   sample return: a spacecraft mission with the intent of gathering samples, such as dirt and rocks, from other celestial bodies for analysis.

2. Students' responses will vary.

3. Students' responses will vary.

4. Diameter of Olympus Mons = 520 km
   Elevation = 20,000 m

5. Diameter of Mt. Rainier = 13 km
   Elevation = 4,200 m

6. Difference in diameter = 507 km
   Difference in elevation = 15,800 km

7. Students' responses will vary.

8. White represents the highest elevation. Dark purple represents the lowest elevation.

Why Whales Migrate (pages 209–210)

1. Students' responses will vary but may include to keep calves safe from predators and for warm, shallow water.

2. Students should draw animals in the food chain in the appropriate order: killer whale, gray whale, amphipods, and phytoplankton.

Answer Key *(cont.)*

3. Students should color high-chlorophyll areas green and low-chlorophyll areas pink and blue and draw an arrow pointing north and label it "Food."

4. Students should draw an arrow south along the migratory route and label it "Temperature."

People Here and There (pages 214–216)

1. Megalopolis: an extremely large city

2. The city lights are only indicators of population distribution because they actually don't reveal any population numbers. They signify more activity in brightly lit areas, but they don't guarantee that these are more populated than others.

3. The highest populations in Egypt are concentrated along the Nile.

4. The coastal regions have more city light activity than the inland areas, particularly the Midwest. The South and East Coast have the most city light activity.

5. The East Coast and West Coast both have a lot of light activity, but there appears to be much more activity on the East Coast.

6. Students should identify a few large cities on each continet.

Overhead Discoveries (pages 220–222)

1.

Location	Size	Indicators	Description
Brazil	415 m (1,350 ft.)	soilmarks, cropmarks	square, angular, lines intersecting, flat

2.

Location	Size	Indicators	Description
Saudi Arabia	70 m (230 ft.)	soilmarks, cropmarks	circular formation with intersecting lines

3.

Location	Size	Indicators	Description
England	340 m (1,110 ft.)	soilmarks, cropmarks	oval shape in a green field

4. Other types of lines include, but are not limited to, roads, rivers, plate boundaries, etc.

5.

Location	Size	Description
Wales	215 km (135 mi.)	shaped like prow of ship, dark lines, under water

6.

Location	Size	Description
Mt. Mabu	9 km (30,000 ft.)	large, green area, mountainous

Assessment Rubric

Use this chart to assess students' technology skills. An example of how to fill it out has been shown here.

Google Earth Skill Assessment Sample

Name: _____

Skill	Cannot Perform	Can Perform with Assistance	Can Perform Independently	Can Use and Apply in Other Situations	Comments
Placemarking			✓		
Create a Path		✓			
Use Ruler Tool				✓	

Assessment Rubric *(cont.)*

Use this chart to assess students' technology skills. Use the blank lines to customize the chart as you want.

Google Earth Skill Assessment Template

Name: _____

Skill	Cannot Perform	Can Perform with Assistance	Can Perform Independently	Can Use and Apply in Other Situations	Comments

How-to Guide

1. Installing and Opening Google Earth

To install Google Earth, go to http://www.earth.google.com and download the latest version. Look for the *.dmg* file on your desktop and click on it. Follow the installation instructions.

To open Google Earth, click on the application. If a pop-up window appears, close it. A view of Earth appears and you are ready to begin.

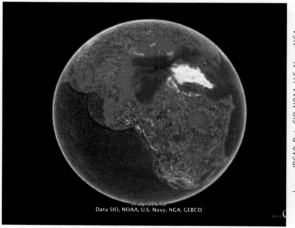

Image IBCAO, Data SIO, NOAA, U.S. Navy, NGA, GEBCO, ©2010 Google

2. Google Earth Window

The **Google Earth Window** includes the **Menu Bar**, the **3D viewer**, the **Toolbar**, and the **Search, Places**, and **Layers Panels**. Within the **3D viewer** are the **Status bar** (at the bottom) and the **navigation tools** (in the upper right). (See page 13 for a full view of the **Google Earth Window** and all the tools, or see Reference.pdf on the Teacher Resource CD.)

3. Google Earth Status Bar

The **Status bar** provides information about the location of the cursor or the center of the **3D viewer**.

Latitude and Longitude: The latitude and longitude (**lat/long**) display in the **Status bar** identifies the coordinates of the cursor, or, if the cursor is off the **3D viewer**, the coordinates at the center of the **3D viewer.**

Elev: The **elev** display represents the elevation, or height of the land relative to sea level at the location of the cursor, or, if the cursor is off the **3D viewer**, the elevation at the center of the **3D viewer.** If the cursor is over the ocean, the elevation is the depth of the ocean.

Eye Alt: **Eye alt** is the height of your eye relative to sea level at the center of the image.

4. Google Earth Navigation Tools

The **navigation tools** allow you to maneuver around the **3D viewer** and to change the **Eye alt** of your view as well as your perspective.

Look Joystick: The **Look joystick** has an eye on it and it allows you to to change your view as if you were moving your eyes. In a close-up view, the arrows allow you to view a mountain or building as if you were standing next to it, looking up and down, left and right. The bottom arrow returns you to an overhead view.

How-to Guide (cont.)

The **North-up button** on the **Look joystick** rotates your view clockwise or counterclockwise. When the Earth is not in a North-up view, click the N on the **North-up button** once to return the Earth to a North-up orientation.

Move Joystick: From a close-up view, the **Move joystick** allows you to move to the north, south, east or west of your current view, depending on which arrow you press. Hold down a section of the circle in the **Move joystick** to fly along above Earth. From a global view, the **Move joystick** rotates the Earth around an axis.

Zoom Slider: The **zoom slider** allows you to change your **Eye alt**, which makes it look like you are zooming in and out of a scene in the **3D viewer.** Click and hold on the **+zoom** to move closer to the surface, or the **–zoom** to move farther away.

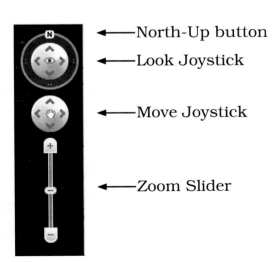

North-Up button

Look Joystick

Move Joystick

Zoom Slider

Street View: Street view allows you to view a region from the level of the street in some locations. **Zoom** in to an **Eye alt** of between 100 and 500 miles until the **Street View pegman icon** appears above the **zoom slider**. Drag the pegman across the **3D viewer** and look for blue lines. Drop the pegman over any of the blue lines and the view will change to a photograph of the view from the street. Use your cursor to drag the image to the left or right to look around, or use the **Move joystick** to move down the road. (**Note:** This imagery is taken from a camera on top of a car; Google™ is building this data set every day.)

5. Google Earth Search, Places and Layers Panels

Search Panel: Use the **Search panel** to find a specific location. Type the location in the **Fly to box** and click the magnifying glass or the return key on your keyboard. Google Earth recognizes the following types of search terms:

- City, state
- City, country
- Number, street, city, state or country
- Zip code or postal code
- Latitude and longitude (**Note:** These should be entered without symbols, but with spaces between degrees, minutes, seconds and cardinal direction, e.g., 72 33 44 N 134 23 45 E)

How-to Guide *(cont.)*

Sometimes a number of options appear under the **Fly to box**. Double-click the one that you are looking for to fly to it directly.

Places Panel: Places that you have searched for can be dragged from the **Search panel** to the **Places panel** using your cursor. Once in the **Places panel**, these places will appear every time you open Google Earth. **Placemarks**, **paths** and **tours,** as well as folders, are stored in the **Places panel** for future reference.

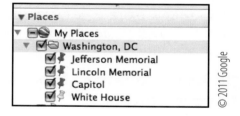

Layers Panel: The **Layers panel** contains a variety of information about Earth in the form of overlays and **placemarks** collected by Google. To see these layers, click the small arrow (Mac) or plus sign (PC) next to **Primary Database** to open the database. Ten layers will appear. Click on the box to the left of each layer turn on the layer and see the overlay or **placemarks** that are contained in that layer. For example, turn on the **Roads layer** to see road lines and names overlaid in Google Earth. When a layer is on, you will see a check mark in the box directly to the left of the layer name. Click the box again to turn the layer off.

If layers have an arrow (Mac) or plus sign (PC) to the left of their names, it means there are additional sublayers available. Click the arrow the plus sign to open the layer menu and see the layers within.

Note: Only keep one or two layers on at a time to prevent Google Earth from slowing down

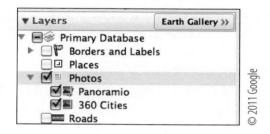

Google Earth is contantly updating the layers data. If any of the layers used in these lessons do not appear in the **Layers panel**, search in the **Google Earth Gallery** for the missing layers.

6. Google Earth Menu Bar

The **Menu Bar**, located at the very top of your computer screen, offers a number of options, some of which are duplicated in the **Toolbar**.

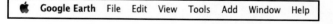

File > Save > Save My Place As: To save a **placemark** or folder, highlight it the **Places panel**. Click **File**, then select **Save** and then **Save My Place As...** to save. A pop-up window will allow you to name the file and

How-to Guide *(cont.)*

choose where to save it. The file is a **.kmz** (keyhole markup language) or **.kml file** named after the computer language used in Google Earth.

Edit > Find: To search for a **placemark** you have previously saved, using a keyword, click **Edit** and select **Find**. In the **Find box** type in a word from the name of a folder or **placemark** that you have saved previously.

View > Grid: To overlay latitude and longitude lines on the Earth, click **View** and select **Grid**. The equator, the Date Line, the Tropics of Cancer and Capricorn, and the Arctic and Antarctic Circles are highlighted.

View > Scale Legend: To add a scale to the lower left corner of the **3D viewer**, click **View** and select **Scale Legend**.

View > Water Surface: To add an artificial water surface over the ocean, click **View** and select **Water Surface**. You can dive below this surface by **zooming** into the ocean and looking up at the surface from below using the **Look joystick**.

7. Google Earth Toolbar

The **Toolbar**, located at the top of the **3D viewer**, allows easy access to a number of tools that can add information to your **3D view.**

Placemark: Save a favorite view as a **placemark** by clicking on the **placemark tool**. In the **Placemark window**, name your **placemark** and add a description. Move the yellow thumbtack cursor in the **3D viewer** to a desired location while the **Placemark window** is open. Click **OK** to save the **placemark**. It will appear either in the **Search panel** or **Places panel**. Drag it to the **Places panel** to save it until the next time you open Google Earth.

To modify or move a **placemark**, right-click (or control-click) on it in the **Places panel**. Select **Get Info** (Mac) or **Properties** (PC) and the **Placemark window** will reappear. You can add a new name or modify the description. Click on the **Style, Color tab** to modify the color and size of the **placemark icon** and label. Choose **View** and use the **navigation tools** to select a new view related to that **placemark**. Click on **Snapshot current view** to keep the new view.

You can change the look of the **placemark icon**. Click on the yellow thumbtack in the upper right corner of the **Placemark window**. A **Placemark icon window** will appear where you can select any number of **placemarks**, or choose **No Icon** if you want to label a **placemark** with a name but not an icon.

How-to Guide *(cont.)*

Placemarks may be collected and organized in folders. At the top of the **Places panel**, right-click (or control-click) on the **My Places** folder and choose **Add**, then **Folder. A New Folder window** will appear that is similar to the placemark window. Type in a ame and click OK. This new folder will appear at the bottom of your list of placemarks in the **Places panel**. Move it to the top of the panel just under **My Places** by dragging it with the cursor. Use the cursor to drag placemarks into this folder. Second and third level folders may be added by right clicking on the first level folder, and then proceeding as above.

Polygon: To create a **polygon** around a feature, click on the **polygon tool** and a **polygon window** will appear. Name the **polygon** and move the cursor (which will be a square) to the first corner of the feature you want to label and click once. Click on the next corner and proceed around the area until all corners are clicked. Click on the **Style, Color Tab** in the **polygon window** and choose a color and an opacity for the lines and the area (100% if you want the lines or area to show up; 0% if you want them to disappear). Click OK.

Path: To create a **path**, click on the **Path tool** in the **Toolbar**. You will see a **path window** and

a square **path cursor** in the **3D viewer**. Name the **path.** Place the **path cursor** over beginning of your desired path and click once. You should see a colored dot. Now move the cursor along your **path** and click again. The first colored dot will turn a different color, and a new colored dot will appear with a line between the two dots. Click several more times to make a four- or five-point path, then click **OK** to close the path window. A **path placemark** will appear in the **Places panel** (or possibly in the **Search panel**) with a path symbol just to its left.

Note that when the **path window** is open, you will need to navigate using the **navigation tools.** Using the cursor will alter your **path**. If you do this accidentally, you can erase the last point on a path by right clicking (or control-clicking) on it.

Tour: To create a tour of several **placemarks**, organize your **placemarks** according how you want to tour them, and click on the **tour tool** in the **Toolbar**. A **record tour panel** will appear in the lower-left corner of the **3D viewer**. The red button on the left is the start/stop button. The numbers indicate the duration of the tour in minutes and seconds (mm:ss).

How-to Guide *(cont.)*

To start a **tour**, click on your first **placemark**, and then click the start/stop button on the **record tour panel**. The entire button will turn red. Wait a second and then double-click on the second **placemark** in your tour. The **3D viewer** will navigate to this placemark. Double-click the third **placemark** and the **3D viewer** will go to this place. Continue to the last **placemark**, then click the start/stop button to stop the **tour**.

A **play tour panel** will appear and the **tour** will automatically start playing. The **play tour panel** includes (from the left) *play, pause, go back, and fast-forward* buttons, a tour slider, an indicator of the current time of the **tour**, a repeat button and a save button. Click the save button to save the **tour**.

Clock: The **clock tool** allows you to look at historical imagery that can go back as far as the 1940s in some locations. Click on the **clock tool** in the **Toolbar** and a **timeline slider** will appear in the upper-left corner of the **3D viewer**. Each vertical bar represents an image that was taken in the past. Use the cursor to move the marker along the **timeline slider** to see these historical images.

Sun: Usually the Earth in the **3D viewer** is entirely lit by the **Sun**. To add a shadow representing the night half of the **Earth**, click on the **sun tool** in the **Toolbar**. A **sun slider** will appear in the upper left corner of the **3D viewer**. Move the slider backwards and forwards to follow the shadows on Earth. Click once on the *sun slider* icon that looks like a magnifying glass with a (–) on it. Notice the time span that is being measured changes (one day, one week, one month, one year). Click on the **sun slider play button** (it looks like a clock with an arrow on it) to watch Earth rotate through the time span on the **sun slider.**

Note that in Google Earth, it appears as though the Sun revolves around Earth, when in reality, Earth revolves around the Sun in a year and rotates around its own axis in a day.

Planets: Uncheck all boxes in your **My Places** folder, as well as any open layers in the **Layers panel**. Click on the **planet** icon in the **Toolbar**. Choose *Moon* or *Mars* and proceed to explore these planets as you did Earth. Note that the layers available in the **Layers** panel have changed and allow you to explore the Apollo landing sites for the Moon, and the rover paths for Mars, as well as many other layers.

How-to Guide *(cont.)*

Ruler: To measure a feature in the **3D viewer**, click on the **ruler tool** in the **Toolbar**. In the **Ruler window**, choose your units of length from the drop down menu. Click from one end of a feature you want to measure to the other. A dot will appear at the first click, and as you move the cursor, a yellow line will appear until your next click. The value for length in the **Ruler window** changes as you move the length of the line.

The **ruler tool** also measures heading (an angular direction relative to north). Click on the **Path tab** in the **Ruler window** to measure the length of a **path**.

Email: A view, folder, or **placemark** can be emailed by clicking on the **email tool** in the **Toolbar**. Choose **Graphic of 3D View** to send a *.jpg* image of the current view. Choose **Snapshot of 3D View** to send a **.kmz file**. Choose **Selected Placemark/Folder** to send a **.kmz file** of a selected **placemark** or folder. Click **OK** and you will be directed to your email application. *Note:* In advance of using the **email tool**, you will need to go to **Preferences** under Google Earth in the **Menu Bar**, and select your email program under the **General tab**.

Print: To print an image from Google Earth, go to the **print tool** in the **Toolbar**. Choose **Graphic of 3D View** and then **Screen**, **Low**, or **Medium** to choose the resolution of your print. Then click **Print**. *Note:* The dimensions next to the print options depend on the dimensions of the **Google Earth Window** open on your screen. Note that printing can be very expensive due to the cost of ink.

Google Earth Skills Matrix

Lesson Title	Google Earth Skill Used
Flying and Finding Earth (page 31)	• **Look joystick** • **Move joystick** • **North-up button** • **Zoom slider**
Searching for Schools (page 37)	• **Search panel: Fly to box**
Placemarking Egypt (page 43)	• **Places panel: Folders** • **Toolbar: Placemark**
Layering Landmarks (page 49)	• **Layers panel: 3D Buildings** • **Layers panel: Photos** • **Layers panel: Roads** • **Layers panel: More: Wikipedia** • Toolbar: Placemark
Identifying Artificial Geographic Features (page 55)	• Layers panel: 3D Buildings • Layers panel: Roads • **Status bar: Eye alt** • Toolbar: Placemark
Investigating Natural Geographic Features (page 61)	• Toolbar: Placemark • Status bar: Eye alt • **Status bar: elev**
Overlaying Abstract Geographic Features (page 67)	• **Fly to box: lat/long** • Status bar: Eye alt • **Status bar: lat/long** • **View: Grid**
Constructing Reference Scales (page 73)	• **Toolbar: Ruler** • View: Scale Legend
Sorting with Folders (page 79)	• Places panel: Folders

Note: Bold indicates the lesson in which a tool is introduced and in which directions for its use are included.

Google Earth Skills Matrix *(cont.)*

Lesson Title	Google Earth Skill Used
Planning an Imaginary Trip (page 85)	• Layers panel: Borders and Labels • **Layers panel: Gallery: Travel and Tourism** • **Layers panel: More: Parks/Recreation Areas** • **Layers panel: Weather: Conditions and Forecasts** • Toolbar: Placemark
Making Literature and Social Studies Connections (page 91)	• **File: Save** • Layers panel: Borders and Labels • Places panel: Temporary Places • Status bar: Eye alt • Toolbar: Placemark • **.kmz file**
Connecting Science and Mathematics (page 97)	• Fly to box: lat/long • Status bar: Eye alt • **Toolbar: Clock** • Toolbar: Placemark, Ruler
Charting the Setting of a Book (page 103)	• Status bar: Eye alt • **Toolbar: Placemark: Description** • Toolbar: Ruler
Watching Events Unfold (page 109)	• Layers panel: Borders and Labels • Layers panel: Roads • Toolbar: Path • Toolbar: Placemark
Touring a Book (page 115)	• Layers panel: Borders and Labels • Toolbar: Placemark • **Toolbar: Tour**
Creating a Book Report (page 121)	• Toolbar: Placemark • Toolbar: Tour: Audio
Experiencing the News (page 127)	• **File: Save: Save Image** • Layers panel: Weather • Toolbar: Clock

Google Earth Skills Matrix *(cont.)*

Lesson Title	Google Earth Skill Used
Tracking Pizarro (page 133)	• Layers: 3D Buildings • Toolbar: Placemark, Ruler, Tour
Mapping the Roman Empire (page 139)	• **Layers panel: Gallery: Ancient Rome 3D** • **Layers panel: Gallery: Rumsey Historical Maps** • Status bar: Eye alt
Going Back in Time (page 145)	• Layers panel: Photos • Layers panel: More: Wikipedia • Toolbar: Clock, Placemark
Inspecting Icy Climates (page 151)	• **Earth Gallery: Arctic Sea Ice**
Colliding Plates (page 157)	• Layers panel: Borders and Labels • **Layers panel: Gallery: Earthquakes, Volcanoes**
Shading the Earth (page 163)	• Status bar: Eye alt • **Toolbar: Sun** • View: Grid
Using Energy (page 169)	• Toolbar: Clock, Placemark • Layers panel: Borders and Labels, Roads • **Layers panel: Global Awareness: Appalachian Mountaintop Removal**
Measuring America (page 175)	• Status bar: Eye alt • **Toolbar: Polygon** • Toolbar: Placemark, Ruler
Building a Capital (page 181)	• Layers panel: Borders and Labels, Places • Status bar: Eye alt • Toolbar: Placemark, Polygon, Ruler
Adding Up Algebra (page 187)	• Status bar: elev • Toolbar: Ruler
Subtracting the Amazon (page 193)	• **Layers panel: Global Awareness: UNEP: Atlas of Our Changing Environment** • Status bar: Eye alt • Toolbar: Polygon

Google Earth Skills Matrix *(cont.)*

Lesson Title	Google Earth Skill Used
Exploring Mars (page 189)	• Fly to box: lat/long • **Layers panel: Featured Satellite Images** • **Layers panel: Global Maps: Colorized Terrain** • **Layers panel: Mars Gallery: Rovers and Landers** • Status bar: Eye alt • **Toolbar: Planets: Mars**
Migrating with Whales (page 205)	• **Earth Gallery: Chlorophyll** • **Earth Gallery: Sea Surface Temperature**
Observing Population (page 211)	• Layers panel: Borders and Labels • **Layers panel: Gallery: NASA: Earth City Lights**
Discovering Places (page 217)	• Fly to box: lat/long • Status bar: Eye alt • Toolbar: Ruler

Recommended Literature

Alcott, Louisa. *Little Women*. Mobile: Roberts Brothers. 1880.

Arthus-Bertrand, Yann. *Earth From Above for Young Readers*. New York: Harry N. Abrams. 2002.

Arthus-Bertrand, Yann. *Earth From Above*. New York: Harry N. Abrams. 2010.

Banyai, Istvan. *Zoom*. London: Puffin Books. 1998.

Brink, Carol. *Caddie Woodlawn*. New York: Simon and Schuster. 2007.

Bruchac, Joseph. *Code Talker: A Novel About the Navajo Marines of World War Two*. New York: Dial Books. 2005.

Campbell, Norman. *Anne of Green Gables*. New York: Samuel French, Inc. 1970.

Choldenko, Gennifer. *Al Capone Does My Shirts*. Logan: Perfection Learning. 2006.

Clark, Ann. *Secret of the Andes*. London: Puffin Books. 1976.

Cole, Stephen and Gardner, Louise. *Cars on Mars*. London: Levinson Children's Books, Ltd. 1997.

Cooper, James. *The Last of the Mohicans*. New York: Penguin Group. 1986.

Creech, Sharon. *The Wanderer*. New York: HarperCollins. 2002.

Curtis, Christopher. *The Watsons Go to Birmingham*. New York: Random House Digitial, Inc. 1997.

George, Jean. *Julie and the Wolves*. New York: Open Road Media. 2001.

Heyerdahl, Thor. *Kon tiki*. Chicago: Rand McNally. 1950.

Holling, Holling. *Minn of the Mississippi*. Orlando: Houghton Mifflin Harcourt: 1951.

Houston, Jeanne and Houston, James. *Farewell to Manzanar: A True Story of Japanese American Experience During and After the World War II Internment*. Orlando: Houghton Mifflin Harcourt. 2002.

Kipling, Rudyard. *Captains Courageous*. New York: Doubleday, Page & Co. 1897.

Kipling, Rudyard. *Captains Courageous*. New York: McMillan & Co. 1897.

Klages, Ellen. *The Green Glass Sea*. New York: Penguin. 2008.

Konigsburg, Elaine. *From the Mixed Up Files of Mrs. Basil E. Frankweiler*. New York: Simon and Schuster. 2007.

Linklater, Andro. *Measuring America*. New York: Penguin. 2003.

London, Jack. *Call of the Wild*. New York: Grosset and Dunlap. 1903.

Lowry, Lois. *Number the Stars*. New York: Laurel Leaf. 1998.

McGraw, Eloise. *Mara, Daughter of the Nile*. London: Puffin Books. 1985.

McGraw, Eloise. *The Golden Goblet*. London: Puffin Books. 1986.

Meigs, Cornelia. *Invincible Louisa*. New York: Little, Brown and Company. 1995.

Morris, Neil. *Volcanoes*. New York: Crabtree Publishing, Co. 1995.

Mortenson, Greg and Relin, David. *Three Cups of Tea*. New York: Penguin. 2006.

North, Sterling. *Rascal*. London: Puffin

Recommended Literature *(cont.)*

Books. 2005.

O' Dell, Scott. *Black Pearl*. Orlando: Houghton Mifflin Harcourt. 1967.

O'Brien, Robert. *Mrs. Frisby and the Rats of NIMH*. New York: Penguin Group. 2011.

O'dell, Scott. *Island of the Blue Dolphins*. New York: Yearling Books. 1987.

Paterson, Katherine. *Bridge to Terabithia*. New York: HarperCollins. 2006.

Peck, Richard. *A Long Way from Chicago*. Pittsburg: Paw Prints Press. 2008.

Peck, Richard. *A Year Down Yonder*. New York: Penguin. 2002.

Pene du Bois, William. *Twenty One Balloons*. London: Puffin Books. 1986.

Publishing, Dorling Kindersley. *Geography of the World*. New York: DK Children. 2006.

Robinet, Harriette. *Forty Acres and Maybe a Mule*. New York: Simon and Schuster. 2000.

Rose, Susana. *Volcano and Earthquake*. New York: DK Publishing, Inc. 2008.

Rylant, Cynthia. *Missing May*. New York: Scholastic, Inc. 1992.

Speare, Elizabeth. *Sign of the Beaver*. Orlando: Houghton Mifflin Harcourt. 1983.

Speare, Elizabeth. *The Witch of Blackbird Pond*. Orlando: Houghton Mifflin Harcourt. 2011.

Sperry, Armstrong. *Call it Courage*. New York: McMillan Press. 1941.

Sperry, Armstrong. *Call It Courage*. New York: Simon and Schuster. 2008.

Stanley, Diane. *Cleopatra*. Madison: Demco Media. 1997.

Stead, Rebecca. *When You Reach Me*. New York: Random House, Inc. 2010.

Stevenson, Robert. *Kidnapped*. London: Cassell. 1886.

Stevenson, Robert. *Treasure Island*. New York: Little, Brown and Company. 1883.

Stintetos, Lorraine. *Misty of Chincotique*. New York: Learning Links. 1995.

Verne, Jules. *20,000 Leagues Under the Sea*. Fairford: Echo Library. 2007.

Verne, Jules. *Around the World in 80 Days*. Charleston: Forgotten Books. 1982.

Verne, Jules. *From the Earth to the Moon*. New York: Scribner. 1890.

Young, Rosalind. *Mutiny of the Bounty and Story of Pitcairn Island*. New York: Little, Brown and Company. 1932.

Glossary of Terms

abstract—not concrete or real

accumulate—gather together or layer on top of, as in snow on a glacier

advance—move forward

align—place or arrange things in a straight line

altitude—height above sea-level

amenities—desirable or useful features or facilities of a building or place

amphipods—any of a large group of small crustaceansthat live in aquatic environments

aquifer—a geological formation, usually underground, that contains groundwater

axis of rotation—the center around which something rotates

axis—a straight line about which a body or geometric object rotates or may be conceived to rotate

biome—a major type of ecological community

breaches—makes a gap in and breaks through

category—a class or division of people or things regarded as having particular shared characteristics

chronologically—in range in order of time of occurrence

circumference—the size of something as given by the distance around it

co-registered—matched

composite—a thing made up of several

compressed—squeezed or pressed together

conquest—to gain or acquire by force

conquistador—a conqueror, especially one of the Spanish conquerors of Mexico and Peru in the 16th century

converge—come from different directions and eventually meet

converged—come together from different places and meet

convergent—moving toward each other

correction—a jog in the road to correct for converging longitude lines

debris—scattered fragments, typically of something wrecked or destroyed

declination—the angle between magnetic north and true north

decompose—decay or become rotten

deforestation—the action of clearing an area of forest

delta—a sediment-filled landform at the mouth of a river where river water flows over the land

dense—closely compacted

diatoms—a major group of algae and one of the most common types of phytoplankton

divergent—moving farther apart

ecosystem—a biological environment consisting of all the organisms living in a particular area, and the physical components such as air, soil, water, and sunlight

electric—operated by electricity

erosion—the process that breaks down rocks (weathering) and the process that carries the broken down rocks

false color—color in an image of an object that does not actually appear in the object but is used to enhance, contrast, or distinguish details

Glossary of Terms *(cont.)*

fertile—capable of producing a large amount of produce

fish trap—ancient contraption designed to capture fish behind a stone wall as the tide flowed out

floodplain—flat land adjacent to a river that stretches from the banks of the river to the base of the enclosing valley walls, and experiences flooding during high water

fly by—a flight past a point, especially the close approach of a spacecraft to a planet or moon for observation

food chain—a series of organisms in which each uses the next usually lower member of the series as a food source

fossil fuels—a natural fuel, such as coal or gas, formed in the geological past from the remains of living organisms

geoglyph—large man-made shapes or designs on Earth that are often indistinguishable from ground level

geographic features—components of a planet that can be referred to as locations, sites, areas, or regions

geyser—a hot spring in which water intermittently boils, sending a tall column of water and steam into the air

glacier—a slowly moving mass or river of ice formed by the accumulation and compaction of snow on mountains or near the poles

Greenwich Mean Time (GMT)—mean solar time at the Royal Observatory in Greenwich, England

heading—an angular direction relative to north

horizon—the apparent line in the distance where the sky meets the sea or land

ice sheet—a permanent layer of ice covering an extensive tract of land, especially a polar region

iceberg—a large floating mass of ice detached from a glacier or ice sheet and carried out to sea

icon—an image that represents something

impact crater—a crater formed on a planetary surface by the impact of a projectile

inauguration—a formal ceremony to mark the beginning of a leader's term in office

irrigation—supplying dry land with water by means of ditches or pipes

itinerary—a planned route or journey

lander—a spacecraft designed to land on a planet or moon

landform—a physical feature in the Earth's surface

landing exercises—landing practices for an invasion on a beach

latitude—the angular distance of a place north or south of the Earth's equator, usually expressed in degrees and minutes

lede—the introduction of a news story

longitude—the angular distance of a place east or west of the meridian

magma—fluid or semifluid material below or within Earth's crust from which lava and other igneous rock is formed by cooling

Glossary of Terms *(cont.)*

megalopolis—a very large, heavily populated city or urban complex or a chain of continuous metropolitan areas

migrate—to pass usually periodically from one region or climate to another for feeding or breeding

moraine—a mass of rocks and sediment deposited by a glacier, typically as ridges at its edges or extremity

mosaicked—combined to form a picture or pattern, like a puzzle

municipal—relating to a city or town or its governing body

narrate—provide a spoken commentary to accompany a movie, book, play, broadcast, piece of music, etc.

navigate—to direct the movement (of the Google Earth view in this case)

Nazca Lines—large animal and abstract geoglyphs made from rocks in a desert in northern Peru

nonrenewable—natural resources that cannot be replaced by natural processes

orbiter—a spacecraft designed to go into orbit around a planet or moon

phytoplankton—microscopic plants that live in the ocean

pivot—the central point, pin, or shaft on which a mechanism turns

provisions—supplies for a trip**radius**—a straight line from the center to the circumference of a circle or sphere

reef—coral feature lying beneath the surface of the water

reference—an indicator that orients you generally

renewable—natural resources capable of being replaced by natural processes

reservation—an area of land managed by a Native American tribe

retreat—the process of receding from a position

revolve—to move in an orbit

rhombus—a parallelogram with four equal sides

rotate—to turn about an axis

rover—a remotely operated vehicle used to explore the terrain of a planet or moon

rural—related to the countryside rather than a city

salt pan—a shallow depression in the ground from which salt water evaporates to leave a deposit of salt

sample return—a spacecraft mission with the goal of returning tangible samples from a location to Earth for analysis

scale—relative size of something

sea ice—frozen sea water on the ocean's surface

sea level—the average level of the ocean's surface

seamount—an underwater mountain rising from the ocean floor

section—a one mile by one mile area of surveyed land in the United States

shoal water—a shallow place in a body of water with a sand bank

sparse—not dense, thinly distributed

spatial—of or pertaining to space

stadium—a sports arena with tiers of seats for spectators

Glossary of Terms *(cont.)*

suburban—related to a town near a big city

surveyor—one whose profession is the surveying of land

tectonics—the study of the Earth's structural features

terrain—vertical or horizontal dimension of the land

thematic—relating to a particular subject

topography—the three-dimensional arrangement of the natural features on a planet or moon's surface

transform—a type of fault for which the plates move horizontally relative to each other

travelogue—a movie, book, or illustrated lecture about the places visited and experiences encountered by a traveler

trench—depression in the ground—in this case created at the boundary between two tectonic plates

trifle—a little bit

tropical—a dense forest occurring in the tropics or near the Equator

tsunami—a long, high sea wave caused by an earthquake or other disturbance

urban—related to a big city

wade—to walk through water

Contents of Teacher Resource CD

Teacher Resources	
Resource	**File Name**
Recommended Literature	Literature.pdf
Google Earth Reference Window	Reference.pdf
How-to Guide	How_to.pdf
Assessment Rubric for Technology Skills	Tech_Rubric.pdf
Student Activity Sheets	
Learning to Fly	
Looking Down	page34.pdf
Schools Around the World	page41.pdf
The Gift of the Nile	page46.pdf
Cultural Symbols	page52.pdf
Seeing Earth	
Artificial Evidence	page58.pdf
An Elevated View	page64.pdf
Latitude and Longitude Lines	page70.pdf
In Scale	page77.pdf
Building My World	
Sorting My World	page82.pdf
Travel Time!	page88.pdf
Islands of War	page94.pdf
Circles	page101.pdf
Language Arts	
On the River	page107.pdf
Walk Two Moons	page112.pdf
Living History	page118.pdf
My Preview	page124.pdf

Contents of Teacher Resource CD *(cont.)*

Social Studies	
Making Memories	page130.pdf
Pizarro's Journey	page136.pdf
Roman News	page142.pdf
The Olympic Games	page148.pdf
Science	
Glaciers and Sea Ice	page155.pdf
Volcanoes	page160.pdf
As the World Turns	page166.pdf
Energy to Burn	page173.pdf
Mathematics	
Plots of Land	page179.pdf
A Capital Idea	page184.pdf
Park Ranger Notebook	page190.pdf
Deforestation	page197.pdf
Interdisciplinary	
Mars	page203.pdf
Why Whales Migrate	page209.pdf
People Here and There	page214.pdf
Overhead Discoveries	page220.pdf

Notes

Notes